FINDING YOUR OWN
SPIRITUAL PATH

FINDING YOUR OWN SPIRITUAL PATH

AN EVERYDAY GUIDEBOOK

Peg Thompson, Ph.D.

Hazelden
Center City, Minnesota 55012-0176
©1994 by Peg Thompson
All rights reserved. Published 1994
Printed in the United States of America
No portion of this publication may be reproduced in any
manner without the written permission of the publisher

Library of Congress Cataloging In Publication Data
Thompson, Peg.
    Finding your own spiritual path : an everyday guidebook / Peg
Thompson.
        p.   cm.
    Includes bibliographical references.
    ISBN 0-89486-912-4 : $12.00
    1. Spiritual life. 2. Non church-affiliated people—Spiritual life.
    I. Title.
BL624.T46 1994
291.4'4—dc20   94-13233
                                                          CIP

All the stories in this book are based on actual experiences. The names
and details have been changed to protect the privacy of the people
involved. In some cases, composites have been created.

CONTENTS

ACKNOWLEDGMENTS

In the back window of my old VW bus a yellow bumper sticker proclaims: GRACE HAPPENS. During the time I have been writing this book, grace has happened in my life literally hundreds of times. Hardly a day has passed without someone asking about my writing or promising me thoughts or prayers. These daily remembrances renewed my spirit and steadied my belief in the value of my work. I thank everyone who gave them to me.

I am thankful to those for whom I have been psychotherapist, spiritual director, supervisor, and consultant. You have taught me, every one of you. I hope this book honors both your struggles and your triumphs.

I thank from the bottom of my heart those women and men who allowed me to interview them as I struggled to frame some of the chapters. Your stories touched me deeply and helped me to put into words ideas barely formed in my mind.

To the congregations and clergy of the Kirk of Bonnie Brae and First Plymouth churches in Denver, and to those of St. Stephen's, Plymouth Congregational, and Spirit of the Lakes churches in Minneapolis, I am grateful.

I thank Marilyn Mason, Richard Solly, and Roseann Lloyd for their advice and enthusiasm as they mentored me through the process of finding and working with a publisher.

Marilyn Frost's encouragement made it possible for me to speak with my own voice, thus becoming an author rather than a scholar.

Kathleen Michels' clarity and attention to detail brought my writing into focus. Her personal warmth and respect gave new energy to my writing.

Barbara Preston's word processing skills saved me from almost certain insanity in the last few months of preparing the manuscript.

I am grateful to Judy Delaney, my editor at Hazelden, for all she did to make this book more inclusive and more accessible.

I give thanks for my relationship with Dan Fourré, my first "soul friend," whose last of many gifts to me was to make for me a straight path to Mary White. I am grateful to Mary for her respectful, caring, and dependable spiritual guidance early in my recovery. And I thank Elizabeth Toohey for her intuitive, affirming, and loving companionship on more recent legs of my spiritual journey.

I am indebted to my friends, who have celebrated with me and consoled me. Their experiences, ideas, and comments have improved the book immeasurably. Thank you especially to Pam Berkwitz, Larry Demarest, Liz Kerwin, Susan McAllister, and Kay Vander Vort.

To write this book I had to dive deeply into the pain of my family experiences. Unexpectedly, at the bottom of that pool of our common suffering, I discovered some of the strengths of my family, both then and now. My parents, Virginia and John, raised me in religious communities that did not wound me in any way—a gift of inestimable value. I am indebted for their daily fostering of my connection with the natural world when I was a child, for it was then and is now the primary dwelling place of my spirit. Their creation and maintenance of the many rituals in our family life gave me a sense of belonging to both the human community and the cosmos. Finally, I am grateful to them for giving me, each in their own way, the competence and the confidence to go my own way—even though they didn't always like the ways I chose to go!

Ron Johnson and Marilyn Peterson, my friends and colleagues at Solstice, have given me a nearly ideal combination of support and independence. Their steadfast care for me as a person, therapist, spiritual director, and writer has been more than anyone could wish for.

My partner Mary Kay's unstinting faith in me and in this project got me through innumerable rough spots. She listened to my doubts and fears and helped me find my voice when it had escaped. She also provided me with the essentials for keeping body and soul together during these past two years: hugs, spaghetti pie, sweets, prayers, flowers, cartoons—and scratch paper!

And to the Great Spirit, the source of all these blessings, and of the dreams that so often guided me, I bow in love and thanksgiving.

— *Winter Solstice, 1992*

The following publishers have generously given permission to use extended quotations from copyrighted works.

From *The Journey Is Home,* by Nelle Morton. Copyright ©1985 by Nelle Morton. Reprinted by permission of Beacon Press. From *The Feminine Face of God: The Unfolding of the Sacred in Women,* by Sherry Ruth Anderson and Patricia Hopkins. Copyright ©1991 by Sherry Anderson and Patricia Hopkins. Reprinted by permission of Bantam Books, a division of Bantam, Doubleday, Dell Publishing Group, Inc. From *Finding God in the World,* by Avery Brooke. Copyright ©1989 by Avery Brooke. Reprinted by permission of HarperCollins Publishers. From *The Sacred Journey,* by Frederick Buechner. Copyright ©1982 by Frederick Buechner. Reprinted by permission of HarperCollins Publishers. From *Telling Secrets,* by Frederick Buechner. Copyright ©1991 by Frederick Buechner. Reprinted by permission of HarperCollins Publishers. From an interview with Robert Coles, broadcast December 25, 1990. Reprinted courtesy of MacNeil/Lehrer Productions. Copyright ©1990. All rights reserved. From *An American Childhood,* by Annie Dillard. Copyright ©1987 by Annie Dillard. Reprinted with permission of HarperCollins Publishers. From Chabad Hasid, in *The Search for Meaning: Americans Talk About What They Believe,* edited by Phillip L. Berman. Copyright ©1990 by Phillip L. Berman. Reprinted by permission of Random House, Inc. From *Wintering,* by Diana Kappel-Smith. Copyright ©1984 by Diana Kappel-Smith. Reprinted by permission of Little, Brown and Company. From "Birthing Compassion," by Sue Monk Kidd. First published in *Weavings* (November-December 1990). Copyright ©1990 by Sue Monk Kidd. Reprinted by permission of the author. From *Nine-Headed Dragon River,* by Peter Matthiessen. Copyright ©1985 by Zen Community of New York. Reprinted by arrangement with Shambhala Publications, Inc., 300 Massachusetts Ave., Boston, MA 02115. From *Family Pictures,* by Sue Miller. Copyright ©1990 by Sue Miller. Reprinted with permission of HarperCollins Publishers. From "Reflections on the Isness," by Alfred Painter. In *The Courage to Grow Old,* edited by Phillip L. Berman. Copyright ©1989 by

ACKNOWLEDGMENTS

Center for the Study of Contemporary Belief, P. O. Box 300553, Denver, CO 80203. Reprinted by permission of Ballantine Books. From "Jim Bob," by Gary Phelps. In *The Search for Meaning: Americans Talk About What They Believe,* edited by Phillip L. Berman. Copyright ©1990 by Phillip L. Berman. Reprinted by permission of Ballantine Books. From "A Total Commitment," by Harry Lee Shaw. In *The Courage to Grow Old,* edited by Phillip L. Berman. Copyright ©1989 by Center for the Study of Contemporary Belief, P. O. Box 300553, Denver, CO 80203. Reprinted by permission of Ballantine Books. Reprinted by permission of Random House, Inc. From *Sacred Moments: Experiences of the Transcendent in the Lives of Ordinary Men,* by Richard Solly. To be published by Hazelden 1995. From *Daybook: The Journal of an Artist,* by Anne Truitt. Copyright ©1982 by Anne Truitt. Reprinted by permission of Pantheon Books. From *One Generation After,* by Elie Wiesel. Copyright ©1970 by Elie Wiesel. Reprinted by permission of Random House, Inc.

1.

BEGINNING THE JOURNEY

Whether you be sleeping or waking, by night and by day, the seed sprouts and grows, though you know not.
—*Rule of Taize*

At some point, most of us were on a spiritual path—we felt connected to the sacred. As children, we may have experienced the divine in singing, in nature, or in friendship. Or we may have felt connected to God when we learned Bible stories or participated in the rituals of our family's religious tradition.

But somewhere in life, many of us lost our way spiritually. Some of us just wandered away from our spiritual life. Attracted to relationships or a career path, we put our energy into building a livelihood and choosing a lifestyle.

Others of us found ourselves on a spiritual path that no longer seemed to be leading anywhere. We may have outgrown our childhood religious upbringing or found its doctrines lacked meaning for us as we learned more about life.

Some of us chose to leave the path because we had been harmed by religious beliefs or religious communities. Angry and self-protective, we escaped religion but inadvertently lost our way spiritually as well.

For many of us, the obstacles to walking a spiritual path are linked with abuse or trauma we suffered as children. Wounded by abuse, we may have been unable to participate fully in religious or spiritual activities. We may have felt unworthy to be cared for by God. Or we may have felt betrayed when God did not hear our prayers for change or rescue.

As children, we learned about God and the life of the spirit from the outside in, usually through religious training. Most of us had spiritual experiences that were independent of religion, but few of us received recognition of the importance of those experiences. We may even have needed to hide our spiritual life to keep it from being trivialized or taken away.

As adults seeking our own spiritual path, it is tempting to follow the same process and to search again from the outside in. For example, we may visit churches, temples, and meditation centers, hoping to find a ready-made path that will fit for us. Often what we encounter leaves us feeling disappointed and disillusioned instead.

In this book I invite you to try something different: seeking your own spiritual path from the inside out. You will still experiment with communities, ritual, and prayer; but instead of focusing on externals, you will be guided to look within. There you will find a wealth of knowledge and wisdom that can direct you as you rediscover your unique connection with the divine. This book will help you reclaim and tell your own story of connection with the sacred, from your earliest recollections to the present. It will help you name and heal the effects of events that frayed or broke the connection. As you know, speak, and write your story, you will find yourself on a spiritual path that is uniquely your own.

It takes a good measure of courage to enter the process of spiritual exploration. As we tell our story, we may be unexpectedly confronted with painful memories, difficult emotions, or menacing images of God left over from childhood. As we become more connected with the sacred in life, we may find that we have to question religious beliefs, experiences, and people in fundamental ways. We may need to grapple with concepts or doctrines that we would rather forget, or face periods of confusion or emptiness.

You may ask, "Why would anyone want to go through this?" We all have our own reasons, reasons that we may not even be able to put into words. Some of us may find that spiritual themes begin to surface gently and spontaneously in our lives, seeming to beckon us into new discovery. Others of us may begin to feel that although we are successful and settled, something is missing in our lives. Some have a jarring experience—the death of someone close to us, a serious illness, an accident, a powerful dream—that plunges us into spiritual questions and dilemmas. A plateau or relapse in recovery may signal our need to expand our spiritual understanding. Or we may find ourselves filled with longing or hunger for a deeper connection with the sacred, an inner directive so compelling that it must be obeyed despite our fears and reservations.

It is hard to tell if we choose to embark on a spiritual journey or if we are nudged onto the path by divine energy. In either case, all of us have times in our lives when spiritual growth is needed if we are to continue to grow and thrive. If we refuse the call, we will be less than our true selves. Having committed ourselves to personal growth, we have also committed ourselves to authenticity—to living out our lives as honestly as we can. It is this commitment that makes us say yes to even the most difficult aspects of spiritual exploration.

A NOTE ABOUT LANGUAGE AND SPIRITUALITY

As we begin the process of exploring our spiritual life, language plays a critical role because it allows us to describe and share our experiences. At the same time, our encounters with the transcendent cannot be completely captured in words.

Conventional religious language may conflict with our personal understanding of the sacred. For example, some people find that language which assumes the existence of a personal God closes them down. Others discover that constant reference to the divine as "He" angers or alienates them. You will probably need to search out a new spiritual language, one that reflects your experiences of the divine.

3

In this book I have used a variety of terms for the sacred. Some you may find familiar and comfortable; others you may find strange or abrasive. As you read, try to notice and value your responses to my language. How do you feel when the sacred is called Higher Power? God? Goddess? The divine? Are you angry, sad, afraid, at peace? Do you feel discounted, validated, encouraged, alienated? If you have strong reactions, let them become the raw material for your reflections or journaling. They will help you hear the voice of your spirit.

I have chosen to use an inclusive language rather than the predominantly masculine language of our culture to describe the sacred. You may find this a breath of fresh air or a profound disturbance. Focus on your reaction and let it tell you something about your relationship with the sacred.

Sharing My Story

My own search for an adult spiritual path began when I was in my late thirties. It was a time when the values that I held most strongly were not at the center of my life. I felt adrift, confused, angry, and frightened. It was also a time of great upheaval in my relationship with my partner, an upheaval which told me clearly that I must change but left me directionless.

I would say that this book began the day I went to my first Al-Anon meeting. The meeting was on the Eleventh Step: "We sought through prayer and meditation to improve our conscious contact with God, asking only for knowledge of God's will and the power to carry it out." When I came to the meeting, I was estranged from religion and cut off from my own spirituality without even knowing it. I was not at all sure I believed in God, but I was certain that I did *not* believe in God's will. Yet, desperate for a change in my life, I found myself thinking, *There's no way I can pray right now. I don't even know who I would be praying to. Maybe I can try meditation.*

Some days later, I went to a large bookstore looking for books on meditation. The very first one I took off the shelf was Stephen Levine's *A Gradual Awakening*. In it were scripts that taught me a way to meditate, and I began to use them.

So began my journey toward writing this book. My faith at this time was in myself, especially in my ability to work through things. Work was a core concept in my worldview. I worked on my primary relationship and my friendships. I worked hard to develop my skills as a therapist.

I placed my faith in my ability to change—to change myself and others. Having grown up in a family in which members did not change even when they were being profoundly wounded by their own behavior, I was determined not to repeat the pattern. I gained a sense of mastery as I learned how to change my own behavior. However, I damaged some of my relationships with my assumption that if only others would change too, I would be happy.

Naturally, my approach to Al-Anon was to work the program in such a way that I could change. Just as naturally, the approach I took to my spiritual life was to work on it. I brought my considerable intensity and self-discipline to the task. I began a daily meditation practice to which I adhered quite diligently.

Then something unexpected happened. Though my meditation was not very quiet or centered, I noticed that the practice was changing me—this despite the fact that, in my opinion, I was not "improving." Even though I was not achieving my goal of stillness in meditation, I was better able to observe others without reacting. I was becoming more calm and compassionate without even trying! Something else was changing me—something I could not name—and I was allowing myself to be changed. In my Al-Anon group, a quiet, respectful meeting in which people shared without comment from others, it seemed to me at first that "nothing was happening." Yet over time, I began to notice that I was changing and so were other people. Something was helping us change, something beyond our own efforts. The shell of my faith in work and self-change began to crack; it was not strong enough to hold my emerging faith in something beyond myself.

I began to have a little faith in talking with others. I felt a tentative faith in relationships as a source of change. I put some faith in what I call "process"—the unfolding of events and relationships that naturally brings about healing and new vitality. I began to have faith in practice—the practice of meditation, the practice of listening, the practice of attending meetings.

In subtle and often unconscious ways, I let my life and the people in it change me. A part of me was afraid of these changes, because I was not in control of them and because being close to other people had sometimes felt unsafe for me in my childhood. Nonetheless, my evolution continued, very slowly, throughout the next few years. Gradually, my faith came to center around an unnamed source beyond myself, a source that I experienced in meditation, in conversation, and in my relationships. I did not think of this source as God or name it God. For me, God was associated with organized religion—with doctrines I did not believe in, with rules of behavior that did not fit for me, and with the oppression of women and gay men and lesbians, which I found intolerable.

This period of fairly serene growth ended abruptly. The egg had cracked before, but this was a Humpty-Dumpty experience. I was seized by a longing to have a more intimate, personal relationship with what I could only call God. No one could have been more surprised by this than I! Throughout my spiritual journeying, I had avoided—even disclaimed—a personal God. Yet here I was in the grip of this longing. During the next several months, I was besieged by intense and unrelieved suffering. Everything that had been rewarding and meaningful seemed shallow. I felt empty. The intensity of my hunger dwarfed the fragile sense of faith that had been emerging over the past few years.

Realizing that I could not find my way through this on my own, I began to look for someone who could help me. Through a series of "coincidences," I began to see a spiritual director. We met once every couple of weeks and talked reflectively about both my longing and my overwhelming fear of being close to the spiritual presence that was calling to me so powerfully.

I discovered that I had two powerful images of God, images that until then had been completely out of my awareness. My first image was of God as a benign but distant being, one that would not hurt me but would not become engaged with me either. Although this God was always present, there was no way I could summon it closer. It was unmoved by either my longing or my suffering. I felt great grief as I explored this image more and more deeply. My other image was of a God who would allow me to come close but when I did would expect the impossible from me: perfection, a heroic mission, an ascetic life. To be close to this God, I would have to give up myself completely. I would be subsumed into "God's plan." I was terrified and full of rage at this dirty trick. I wanted nothing to do with a God who would rob me of my self.

For a period of months I lived with these two God images. I wrote about them and drew them in my journal. I even dreamed about them. Gradually, it became clear that these images arose from some of my childhood experiences with my parents. It was as if God had been hidden in their shadow. Once I recognized them, I was free of my terror and rage. I began to explore how I had been touched by the sacred in my life and what images of God would be true to my experience. I slowly developed a relationship with a more personal divine presence who connects with me in many different ways. This being is moved by my suffering and the suffering of all beings; it is present in listening and talking, in relating, in process and practice; it is the source of change.

For the past ten years, I have had a form of systemic arthritis. It usually is quite mild, but a few years ago I had a major flare-up. During this episode, my fatigue was so intense that I had to severely limit my activity level simply to be able to work and perform the tasks of daily life. Being so sick forced me to face the fact that my sense of identity and self-worth was almost completely tied up with my ability to be active in the world.

Gradually, through conversations with friends and periods of prayer, I began to understand that I have value simply because I am alive. The core of my faith was shifting again, from faith in problem solving to faith in being.

Each of the shifts in my spiritual life has taken several years to become fully a part of me. I know that I have only begun to live out this new sense that I am important and lovable solely because I am alive. I have only begun to know what it means, day to day, to draw primarily on the energy and guidance of the divine and other human beings rather than on my own.

My ten-year search for a connection with the divine has been a gradual process of finding faith and outgrowing it, being given faith and living beyond it, living faith and knowing it will change.

Your journey may be very similar to or very different from mine. You may be able to connect easily with me in some parts and not at all in others. Let yourself know what effect my story has had on you. Do you feel connected or disengaged, enthusiastic or frightened, calm or angry? Your feelings and reactions will be helpful guides to your inner self as you read this book. As you read and reflect, remember that each of us comes to life as an original creation. Your journey to and your experience of the holy is uniquely your own.

SPIRITUALITY AND RELIGION IN MY PROFESSIONAL LIFE

Over the past several years, my clients have taught me that growth in the life of the spirit is essential to recovery. From them, I have learned that each of us finds his or her spiritual path from within. I marvel at the myriad paths on which people find their way to the sacred—and the sacred finds its way to them. And I always have a sense of mystery. Why do they have to struggle so much? Why is God seemingly so far away when they are so much in need? Where will their paths lead?

My first lesson in spiritual development was given to me by a client about a year after I began to meditate and participate in Al-Anon. A recovering alcoholic, this client had been sober a year or so after many years of destructive drinking. She felt stymied in both her recovery program and her therapy because neither was giving her any solid guidance about her spiritual life. She was frightened because she knew she had to make progress or she would eventually go back to drinking. At the end of the session, she said, "So what is this spirituality stuff, anyway?" Nothing in my training had prepared me for this question. I had been taught to make a referral to a cleric if a client had religious issues. And no one in the academic world during the mid-seventies was talking about spirituality! I told my client that I couldn't answer her question and suggested she talk with her AA sponsor about it.

A few months later, she expressed the same frustration—and again a few months after that. She was becoming more fearful and more dispirited. The third time that I said I really did not know anything about spirituality, she retorted angrily, "Don't you think you *should?*" The desperation and fear behind her question touched me deeply. And the answer to it was obvious: Of course I should.

As my own relationship with the sacred grew, I was able to hear the subtle and tentative ways clients were talking about their religious struggles and their spiritual questions and experiences. As I listened, they began to share more and more about their spiritual lives with me. I tried to listen and let them teach me. The more I absorbed from them, the more intense became the pull toward learning more and putting what I was learning into words.

Eventually, the inner imperative I felt became so strong that it seemed I would violate my very spirit not to follow it. I returned to graduate school. In a self-designed program, I studied both spiritual direction and the role of the therapist in relation to religious and spiritual issues. I participated in a supervised practicum as a therapist. I was trained in an internship to offer spiritual direction.

While a student, I began to see a few clients for spiritual direction and to engage with clients more wholeheartedly in exploring the spiritual concerns they brought to therapy. It has been a sacred and life-giving experience for me to be with clients—those for whom I am spiritual director or therapist—and listen with them for the voice of the holy.

ESSENTIALS FOR FOSTERING OUR SPIRITUAL GROWTH

As with any journey, our search for our own spiritual path requires preparation. When we travel, we prepare by planning and gathering everything we will need. If we are to sustain our spiritual journey, there are five essentials we must provide ourselves: kindly self-discipline, safety, an environment of empathy and trust, dialogue, and community.

Paradoxically, these requirements are also the results of spiritual growth. Our self-discipline helps us claim the time and energy we need to explore our connection with the sacred. As we explore, our sense of safety increases. As we grow in self-awareness, our sense of empathy and trust deepens. As we become more willing to share, our community of dialogue expands.

KINDLY SELF-DISCIPLINE

When we prune a tree, we remove small, weak branches to strengthen it. Without pruning, these branches may break off, exposing the tree to life-threatening diseases or insects. In the life of the spirit, self-discipline is like pruning. It directs our energy into some areas and not others. It protects us from pursuing too many activities superficially. It empowers us to move spirituality to a place of priority among our other commitments. It encourages us to grow strong.

What kind of discipline allows us progress on our spiritual path? It is kindly self-discipline—discipline that arises from a sense of care and responsibility for ourselves. Kindly self-discipline honors our internal rhythms, our preferences, our commitments, our energy level, our style of engagement. It assumes our personal worth and meaning. It sees who we are now and envisions who we may become. It meets challenges that enhance our sense of vitality. It is willing to risk and to wait for results. If you have a great deal of difficulty summoning up this kind of discipline, you may find it useful to explore your family's patterns of correcting children's behavior.

In troubled families, discipline may be problematic in three ways. Harsh discipline can create a climate of power in which someone wins at another's expense. Because it focuses on character rather than on behavior, harsh discipline does not allow the child to learn. Inconsistent discipline makes the consequences of any behavior wildly unpredictable. Finally, inadequate discipline creates an environment of chaos, meaninglessness, and even despair.

A family with harsh, inconsistent, or inadequate discipline wounds the spirit by placing outcomes above people. Members are neither seen nor counted; therefore, their very sense of self can be hurt repeatedly. True conversation cannot happen because fear or chaos dominates. Thus, problems with discipline interfere with safety, love and trust, dialogue, and community.

10

Simply knowing what you learned in childhood may free you to go easy on yourself in your journey toward spiritual growth.

SAFETY

Safety provides us with a sheltered environment in which to grow. It allows us to keep our emerging spiritual self from being exposed to harsh or harmful people and experiences. If in our experience safety cannot be assumed, we will find it threatening to open ourselves to the holy. If our spirit is to grow, however, we must find a way to do just that.

Let me suggest two principles that may be helpful. First, you will probably want to find a place to read this book where you can be assured of uninterrupted time for reflection: a restaurant, a library, a cozy spot in your kitchen or den. Experiment until you find a place that feels right for you.

Second, if you decide to use a journal in conjunction with this book, it will be important to ensure that no one else has access to it. Knowing that someone else might read your most personal reflections is inhibiting: you may begin to write what that person wants to hear or will be impressed with; or, expecting criticism or judgment, you may not write all of your truth.

Ensuring your privacy may take some thought and planning. It may simply require telling your partner, children, parents, or others in your home that it is important that your journal be just for you. Some of you may need to find a place to lock up your journal or keep it outside your home.

EMPATHY AND TRUST

As children, we learned how to relate to ourselves from the way our parents and other adults treated us. If they mistrusted us, we learned to doubt ourselves. If they ignored us, we acquired a tendency to neglect ourselves. If they humiliated us, we developed the habit of shaming ourselves. If they criticized us, we learned to scold ourselves.

If this has been your experience, you may treat yourself harshly or be only dimly aware of your inner world. To grow spiritually, you will need to practice listening to your thoughts and feelings without criticism, building up a relationship of empathy as you go.

Empathy allows us to trust ourselves to make decisions in our best interests. We can set a pace and a depth of exploration that do not leave us feeling empty or overwhelmed. We can welcome the unfinished, confused, angry, upset, unruly, and resistant parts of ourselves as indispensable companions on our spiritual journey.

We can also create a climate of empathy and trust by calling up memories of times when we were cared for by loving people. Even those of us with the most violent or neglectful of childhoods nearly always can name at least one such person. It may have been an aunt or uncle, a sibling, a grandparent. It may have been a teacher, a minister, a coach or camp counselor, a neighbor. As adults, we may also have felt cared for by a significant other, therapist, sponsor, friends, family members, or even strangers. The exercise on page 21 provides one way to summon such a memory.

DIALOGUE

Spiritual growth flourishes in dialogue with others.

We may fear dialogue for any number of reasons. If we were silenced in early life, we may not know how to put into words what is in our heart. We may be afraid we will sound childish or inappropriate. We may not believe that we will be heard. We may expect to be condemned. If we come from a family that is rigid about religion, we may anticipate that others will tell us the "right" way. These fears and expectations may cause us to try to journey alone, without talking to others and without hearing their stories.

If traumatized as adults—for example, by rape or battering—we may cut ourselves off from dialogue about spirituality and religion because we feel ashamed. The experience of trauma raises profound questions, questions foreign to people who have not suffered similarly. If we have been the victim of violence or terror, we often feel alone and different. We may fear that dialogue would only heighten our sense of isolation. We may avoid disclosing the shattering of our faith in fear of others' insensitivity or criticism. We may not want to share our innermost feelings about the sacred because they are clouded by despair.

Dialogue has many levels. The most basic is conversation with our self, expressing our thoughts, feelings, and memories in words and listening to them with an attitude of welcome. We are in dialogue when we read books and articles on spirituality or scripture passages, watch television programs, attend lectures, or listen to inspirational tapes. These conversations with "experts," which take place in our inner world, prepare us for interpersonal conversations. From them we learn to know and value what we have to say and to respond to what others tell us.

To thrive, however, we need to talk about our spiritual life with others with whom we feel some degree of safety, empathy, and trust. We then can risk dialogue, sharing a little and seeing how it goes before we share more. Gradually, we experience a feeling of communion with others. Often, this prompts us to seek a community of persons with whom we want to journey.

COMMUNITY

Spiritual communities provide us with models of spiritual seeking. They support our journey and lend us energy when we get stuck. Yet many of us avoid spiritual communities as we begin a renewed spiritual journey. We do so for good reasons. If our childhood religious community was damaging or alienating, we may refuse to have any contact with spiritual communities. We may be enraged by some religious practices. We may feel intruded on by doctrines that dictate what we must believe. We may feel that religious tradition disallows doubt or questioning. If we were not raised in any religious community, we may feel uncertain about how to belong.

Traumatic experiences in adulthood may also leave us angry at or alienated from religious communities. We may feel discounted by pat remedies: "You must forgive and forget" and "God never gives us more than we can handle." We may feel abandoned when church members fail to ask how we are or visit us when we have suffered trauma. We may feel set apart by our experience, unable to connect with people and traditions that once nourished us.

However, most of us reach a point in our journey where we feel that we have gone as far as we can go alone. We become aware of our need for a deeper sense of spiritual identity than that which we can find on a solitary journey. When we feel safe enough, we can allow ourselves to experience the natural desire to share our spirituality in community with others. Belonging to a spiritual community then grows out of our inner longing, not a "should" that comes from outside.

At this point, we can begin to think about what kind of community we need. Fortunately, community is not limited to churches and temples. Millions of people experience Twelve Step groups as spiritual communities. Others find kindred spirits at gatherings where people meet to create rituals for various occasions. Some people meet in informal groups or attend retreats to share their spiritual journey.

Kindly self-discipline, safety, empathy, trust, dialogue, and community foster spiritual growth. We must begin where we are, wherever that is. Small steps will lead to larger steps. Luckily, there is no timetable for healing. There is no hurry; we have a lifetime. The sacred dimension of life is always open to us.

A READER'S GUIDE

Coming to know and understand ourselves in relation to the sacred is a process similar to working a large jigsaw puzzle. In day-to-day life, we use logic, reason, and sequential thought to analyze and solve problems; using that method, we could try to work the puzzle from right to left and top to bottom, one piece at a time, in order. But we all know how nonproductive that would be!

A more fruitful approach would be to call on our intuitive, holistic, and relational abilities, which allow us to see relationships among separate parts and understand how they come together to make a whole. Using this approach to a puzzle, we first would sort out the straight pieces and build the frame. Then we would work on the puzzle in sections, working from the best-defined sections to the least-defined. Eventually the clusters would be large enough for us to make connections between them. Finally, we would fill in the remaining spaces, thus completing the puzzle.

Rarely do we complete a puzzle at one sitting. Usually, we work on it for a while—often until we get stuck—and then take a break for "real" life. When we return, the puzzle is still there—often with some pieces added by other members of the household—and we immediately see where other pieces belong.

Spiritual deepening happens in this way. It starts and stops; it grows as a result of events in our lives when we are not paying attention. It is always there, even when we are involved elsewhere. We can come back to it at any time; there is no hurry. Though we never complete the puzzle, we come to value the working of it as an activity in itself.

In this book informational sections alternate with exercises that allow you to reflect on and write about what you discover. The exercises are designed to allow different people to use them in many ways. I hope you will feel free to use them in the way that fits best for you.

Each chapter has four parts. The first section is an **Introduction**, a framework for exploration.

The second section, **Passageway**, presents various methods of entering the intuitive space where spiritual exploration can occur. It may take some practice to feel at home in this inner space. Be patient with yourself. Adopt an encouraging attitude. If you notice that you're criticizing your performance, gently bring yourself back to a tone of encouragement.

You will probably find that some of the Passageway exercises will work for you very readily, while others may not fit for you at all. If you find a way of entering the exploratory space that works well, feel free to use it as the entry point for other chapters. The Passageway exercises are interchangeable. If an exercise stirs up painful memories or makes you anxious, don't force yourself to use it. Just choose another exercise.

You may find it helpful to record the Passageway exercise on tape. If you do, read it very slowly, leaving generous pauses (suggested by the symbol ◉) as you go. Let your voice be soft and gentle as you record it. If you decide not to tape-record the Passageway, you may read it to yourself silently or aloud as you go.

Next is the **Exploration and Discovery** section. Included here are workbook exercises designed to help you discover more about various aspects of your spiritual life and history. Let them evoke and express your experience in a very personal way. See if you can give yourself permission to put aside all your English teachers' rules about grammar and composition.

The greatest value in this book lies not in the text, but in *your experiences*. While the text will structure your explorations, the discoveries you will make from doing the exercises will place your feet securely on your own path. Understandably, you may be tempted to skip over them to save time or to avoid meeting difficult memories or impasses. But, unless an exercise does not fit for you at all, I encourage you to resist the temptation and dive in.

Finally, each chapter closes with a section called **Reflection and Integration**. Here I invite you to reflect on what you have learned from the chapter as a whole. You may see patterns and relationships that were not apparent before. You may identify growing edges within yourself. You may comment on gaps in the life of your spirit. You may notice strong feelings of anger, grief, joy, or peace. You may find that the material raises new questions for you and/or answers old ones. You may gain access to submerged memories.

To get the most out of this book, you will need a notebook or journal in which you can write about or draw your memories, insights, feelings, and ideas as you read each chapter. I have used the symbol ✍ to signal that you may want to do some journaling or drawing.

Like the produce department in a supermarket, everything in this book has nutritional value, but not everyone needs or relishes the same kinds of food. I hope you will feel free to skip some parts and immerse yourself in others. Since your needs may change over time, you may want to come back to sections that you originally skipped. You may find it fruitful to repeat an exercise after a period of months or years.

At times, though, you may sense that you make your choices out of a kind of resistance. You may notice a feeling of anger or fear when you look over an exercise. It may be useful to take some time to explore these feelings and put them into words. This work may become the real exercise!

All your responses to this book are important. I hope you will notice them as you read and try the exercises. Often, we feel shame if we are angry about prayer, faith, or an image of God. Understandably, we want to avoid pain and terror. However, these feelings, I have found, are the passages to a deep inner life. They deserve our attention and respect. They need to be put into words and spoken aloud. They are integral to your unique story. As you read on, you will probably find that childhood feelings and images lie side by side with adult ones. All aspects of yourself ask to be heard. All have a gift to offer you.

With each chapter, I encourage you to give yourself the time to go deeper rather than faster as you explore. If you are sharing your spiritual journey with others, try to focus on listening, learning, and understanding rather than comparing, competing, or judging.

PASSAGEWAY

When you're ready, find a comfortable spot to sit and write. Remember to bring along this book and your journal. Take whatever time you need to get settled. Then skim the entire Passageway exercise. Decide whether you want to read it silently or aloud or make a tape recording of it. This exercise should take about fifteen minutes.

When you're ready, begin.

Close your eyes and sit quietly for a minute or two. ❦ Gently bring your attention to this place, ❦ to this moment. ❦ Be aware of your surroundings ❦ what you see, ❦ what you hear, ❦ what you smell, ❦ what you taste, ❦ what you feel in your body. ❦

Now use your fingers to block your ears so that you can't hear anything but your own breathing. ❦ Be aware of the silence. ❦ Listen to the sound of your breathing for a few minutes. ❦ Breathing in ❦ and breathing out. ❦ In ❦ and out. ❦ In ❦ and out. ❦

When you feel attuned to your breathing, take your fingers away

17

from your ears. ❧ Notice all the assorted sounds you can hear now. ❧ Bring your attention to them, one by one. ❧ Be aware of the sounds that are closest to you ❧ those that are farther away ❧ and those you can barely hear. ❧ Notice all the sounds that you can hear. ❧ As you do, practice not identifying or naming them. ❧ Just hear exactly how they sound as themselves. ❧ Take a few minutes to notice the qualities of the various sounds. ❧ Listen to their pitch, ❧ loudness, ❧ and length. ❧ Notice sounds within sounds ❧ and how sounds change continuously. ❧ Now be aware of how the sounds blend and separate, ❧ like musical instruments during a symphony, ❧ beginning and ending at different times, ❧ making a whole from many parts. ❧ Take a few minutes to listen to this symphony ❧ and its parts. ❧

Now gently bring your attention back to your surroundings ❧ and to the present moment. ❧ When you are ready, open your eyes.

If you notice the effect of the Passageway fading as you do the exercises that follow, take a few minutes to return to it and then continue.

EXPLORATION AND DISCOVERY

These exercises focus on the essentials for fostering spiritual growth.

KINDLY SELF-DISCIPLINE

Take a few minutes now to relax and focus. Be aware of how you are feeling about the issue of self-discipline. Let your awareness focus on your habits of self-discipline. How do you discipline yourself to do the things that are important to you? How do you feel when you use these approaches? ✍

Now list the five highest priorities in your life in descending order, from most to least important. Where, if at all, does your spiritual recovery fit on this list? ✍

Let yourself know how much time you feel you can realistically give to exploring your spirituality. What time of the day would work best for you? What day or days of the week? Would you prefer to devote large or small blocks of time? Take some time just to sit with these questions and let the answers come to you out of your own life experience. If you wish, make a few notes in your journal about the kind of self-discipline you are thinking of. ✍

SAFETY

1. *A safe place.* Reflect quietly about places where you would feel safe enough to explore your spirituality. Be gentle with yourself and take your time. Use whatever approach works best for you.

   Close your eyes and focus on your breathing for a few minutes. Let yourself relax a little. When the time feels right, let your mind wander through all the rooms in your home. Notice the feelings you have in each room. Then take a few minutes to think of public places you enjoy: perhaps a library, a restaurant, a park. Let your mind linger in each place for a few minutes, tuning in to your feeling of safety or apprehension. If you find a spot that you might use as a base for spiritual exploration, make a note of it. ✍

   Would you like to bring a special object into your safe place? A blanket or shawl, a candle, a favorite stuffed animal, an art object, a photograph, a book? Imagine various objects being present in the place you have chosen. Do they enhance your feeling of safety? Perhaps the place is safe just as it is. ✍

   Now pause for a moment and let yourself feel the quality of the energy in your safe place. Are there any changes you would like to make? When you have it just right, describe the qualities of your safe place and your feelings about it. ✍

   If you have not found a place that feels safe, let yourself know how you feel about not having a spiritual "home." ✍

19

2. *Privacy.* Take a few minutes to reflect on the issue of privacy. Who lives with you or has access to your home? Think about them one by one. Does each have a sense of privacy about his or her own inner life? About others' possessions? If there are children in your home, do they understand the concept of privacy? Do they respect others' personal belongings even when they are at home alone or with their friends? ✍

Is there anyone you need to talk with about your need for your journal to be private? How would it be best to approach him or her? ✍

If for whatever reason you cannot depend on someone to respect your privacy, what steps must you take to ensure it? Make a plan about maintaining your privacy and take a few minutes to jot down the plan in your journal. ✍

EMPATHY AND TRUST

1. *Empathy for self.* The following open-ended statements may help heighten your awareness of the inner environment in which this leg of your spiritual journey will take place. Read through the statements one by one. If one does not elicit anything from you, move on to the next. Then take a few minutes to note your responses in your journal. ✍

- I can/cannot trust myself to know what is best for me on this journey because...
- I feel most open to myself when I am...
- It is hard for me to be open to myself when I am...
- I cannot be truly available to myself until...
- I am/am not in a hurry to make progress on my spiritual journey because...
- To maintain consistent respect for my feelings and needs as I explore my spiritual life, I will need to...

2. *Empathy from others.* A memory of being loved can connect you to your inner world of empathy and trust. You may want to visit it if you feel confused, stuck, or frightened.

Take a moment for reflection now. Do you remember a time when you felt loved by a trusted person, even if only briefly? If you do, notice your feeling of being important and interesting to that person. Now take time to relive this event in detail. What feelings do you have? What do you see and hear? What time of year is it? How old are you? How does your body feel? Let yourself experience for a few minutes all the feelings and sensations of being loved by a trusted person. Try to capture all the details; they will make the experience more immediate for you. ✍

When you finish writing, notice how you're feeling. Give yourself time to return gradually to the present.

DIALOGUE

Take a few minutes to relax and find your reflective inner space. When you are ready, call into your mind, one by one, the important people in your life—spouse or partner, therapist, spiritual director, friends, relatives, work associates, acquaintances. As you do, weigh each of them as a possible partner in dialogue.

Now focus on the person with whom you could most easily share your spiritual journey. Sit quietly with the image of this person for a few minutes. Call to mind your experiences with him or her.

Consider what you might like to share with this person about how you came to begin reading this book. Be aware of how you feel as you imagine talking about it, especially how safe and trusting you feel.

Take a moment to reflect on what you've learned in this exercise. ✍

Note: You may want to repeat this exercise to help you consider other persons with whom you might share.

21

COMMUNITY

If you feel safe enough in your own journey to explore the idea of community in your imagination, you may find this exercise helpful. If you're not ready, I invite you to skip ahead. You can come back later if you wish.

Take a few minutes now to put yourself in a quiet space. Let your body and mind relax. When you are ready, focus your attention on the word *community*. Notice how you feel when you think of community in connection with spirituality. Are you curious? Eager? Afraid? Angry? Delighted? Do you feel a sense of longing? Let yourself know about all of your feelings about community. Be aware of whether you feel a need for community at present. ✍

If you would like to search for or create a community in your life now, take a few minutes to reflect on the people in your life. With whom do you feel a sense of community? Are there any who would gladly support your spiritual or religious life? They may be members of a church or synagogue, a family group, or a group of friends. Let yourself know more about your feelings about them as individuals and as a group. What do you draw from this community? What might it offer you as you explore your spirituality more deeply? What might be its limitations? ✍

As you reflect, you may find that you would like to have a community but not right now. If this is the case, note your feelings about its absence. ✍

REFLECTION AND INTEGRATION

Allow some time to recenter yourself. You may find it easier to refocus if you repeat the Passageway, listen to music, focus on your breathing, have a cup of tea, or take a walk.

Now take a few minutes to look over everything you've written in your journal in connection with this chapter. The trends and themes may become apparent in a fragmentary, nonlinear way. Give yourself permission to write about them as they come. For example, write just one or two words. Cross out an entry if it doesn't feel right. Grope for words. Write sideways on the page. Scribble. Draw instead of write. Let the spirit within you speak in its own voice, whether it be tentative or bold, poetic or prosaic.

You may use any of the following questions (and/or any others you choose) to guide your reflections: ✍

- What strengths and assets do you bring to the process of spiritual exploration?
- What are the challenges you face as you prepare for it?
- What are the conflicts—either within yourself or with others—that may need to be addressed in order for you to continue exploring?
- Who or what will nurture and support you as you proceed?

2.

SPIRITUALITY:

OUR CONNECTION WITH THE SACRED

*I have come to the conclusion along the way that there is such a
thing as the wintering of the human spirit; by spirit I mean the
force which we hold, hidden, chrysalised, at it were, under a
layered shell of physical necessity and present time. The spirit seems
to inhabit no time and no space at all, but it...resounds when
it meets the world, like a tuning fork which has been struck against
the edge of a table. By its sudden music we know it is there.*
                                                    —*Diana Kappel-Smith*

*B*y spirituality, I mean *our inner experience of the sacred and our living
out of that experience.* Nearly everyone has encountered the sacred at
some time. During a time of desperation, we may have seen a radiant rain-
bow or a lush sunset. We may have felt safe in a sacred way when, as children, we sat in a favorite tree or played with a pet. Watching spring come,
we may have been filled with the holiness of that season of renewal.
Listening to a thunderstorm at night, we may have been struck by the
same awe that the sacred invokes.

We may have encountered the sacred in the birth of a child, in a
heartfelt talk with a friend, in a brush with death. Perhaps we felt safe in
a special way on the lap of a trusted parent or grandparent. Maybe we
encountered the holy when we received help from someone or when we
aided a stranger. Perhaps we experienced it in singing or listening to
music during a church service, in feeling deeply touched by a story from
scripture, or in being heard at our core by a member of the clergy.

RECOGNIZING YOUR SPIRITUAL EXPERIENCES

You need only one memory of an encounter with the sacred to continue exploring in this chapter. If you do not have even one such memory, you can skip to the next chapter and come back later. Each of us remembers in our own way. Some people are instantly flooded with the details; others start with only a glimmer that expands with time. Whatever your process, greater awareness will come if you simply pay attention. Give yourself permission to begin where you are and to value the place that belongs only to you. You can trust your inner process to give you what you need.

AWE AND WONDER

The holy fills us with awe and wonder. We become still, hardly breathing. Or we are moved to a quiet inner space. We may glimpse another world that we rarely see, but one that is always there. Often, we feel blessed or lucky.

One woman described such an encounter:

> I was in my mid-twenties, I think. I started going camping alone, with just my dog. It was in the spring, at Cascade River State Park. I was sitting on a little bridge just below a beautiful waterfall. I had a very real sense of blessing. I thought, *This is a miracle.* I felt connected to the creator of such beauty. I had a sense of total personal integration—that this was all part of God and all part of me. I just sat there looking at it and said, "Thank you." I recognized this, even at the time, as an enormously significant event in my life.

Understandably, our awe could be mingled with fear. An authentic encounter with divine energy can force us to confront our powerlessness. A barrage of questions may hit us: What will be expected of me if I reach out to the divine? Will I have to give up my family? Change my career? Will I become eccentric? Will I lose my hard-won sense of identity?

The feeling of wonder often visits us unexpectedly. Richard Solly, in his book *Sacred Moments*, related the experience of Greg, who had been on a deer hunting trip with his father and his brothers:

> After nearly seven hours in the stand, Greg had not sighted a single deer. His feet and hands were cold and numb; his joints stiffened. He was bored and unhappy. "I've had it," he announced to his father as he climbed down....
>
> Dejected, Greg walked back through the woods. He stepped over tree roots and fallen limbs until he saw a clearing twenty yards ahead.
>
> "I remember it exactly," he said "[A] path, probably a deer path, cut straight across the clearing. At first I felt strangely apprehensive because walking out into the open would leave me exposed, but as I came out of the trees...I was suddenly struck by how beautiful it was. It had just started to snow. At first the flakes were small, but then huge snowflakes began coming down, in slow motion!...Each snowflake was perfect. This is difficult to explain but it felt like something was coming down in the snow. A Presence. I was awestruck and I just stood there. I held the rifle and watched snowflakes fall on the gun barrel.... I wasn't cold any longer, and I remember just wanting to stand there. I felt a presence of God, and I was overwhelmed by it.... Tears came to my eyes.[1]

Have you had an encounter with the sacred in which you felt awe and wonder? Make a note about it in your journal if you wish. ✍

ALTERED SENSE OF TIME AND PLACE

When we encounter the sacred, our sense of time and place may be altered. We may see the setting sun subtly change the colors of the sky moment by moment. We may come to the end of an intense talk with a friend and be shocked to find that hours have passed. Deep in meditation or prayer, we may not be aware of the traffic outside. Immersed in a creative project, we may not notice that darkness has fallen.

27

In his book *The Sacred Journey*, Frederick Buechner describes a morning at home. Notice how his sense of this familiar place is changed by the sounds he hears.

> On the wall behind me, an old banjo clock was tick-tocking the time away. Outside I could hear the twitter of swallows as they swooped in and out of the eaves of the barn. Every once in a while, in the distance, a rooster crowed, though it was well past sunup.... In another part of the house two men were doing some carpentry. I could not make out what they were saying, but I was aware of the low rumble of their voices, the muffled sounds of their hammers, and the uneven lengths of silence in between. It was getting on toward noon, and from time to time my stomach growled as it went about its own obscure business which I neither understand nor want to. They were all of them random sounds without any apparent purpose or meaning, and yet as I paused to listen to them, I found myself hearing them with something more than just my ears to the point where they became in some way enormously meaningful. The swallows, the rooster, the workmen, my stomach, all with their elusive rhythms, their harmonies and disharmonies and counterpoint, became, as I listened, the sound of my own life speaking to me. Never had I heard just such a coming together of sounds before, and it is unlikely that I will ever hear them in just the same combination again. Their music was unique and unrepeatable and beyond describing in its freshness.... I was moved by their inexpressible eloquence and suggestiveness, by the sense I had that they were a music rising up out of the mystery of not just my life, but of life itself.[2]

Have you had any experiences of the sacred in which your sense of time and space was out of the ordinary? Make a note of them. ✍

MYSTERY

An encounter with the holy often has an aura of mystery. For example, the solution to a problem that has baffled us for months may suddenly be clear, although we have no idea how it came. Filled with anger and bitterness, we may visit a parent's grave only to leave at peace—and not know why. Finding ourselves lost and alone, we may suddenly feel guided by an invisible companion. Anne Truitt, an artist, writes of her startling encounter with a painting:

> When we rounded into the lowest semicircular gallery, I saw my first Barnett Newman, a universe of blue paint by which I was immediately ravished. My whole self lifted into it. "Enough" was my radiant feeling—for once in my life enough space, enough color. It seemed to me that I had never before been free…. I would not have believed it possible had I not seen it with my own eyes. Such openness wiped out with one swoop all my puny ideas. I staggered out into the street, intoxicated with freedom, lifted into a realm I had not dreamed could be caught into existence. I was completely taken by surprise, the more so as I had only earlier that day been thinking…my life as a human being [was] complete.
>
> I stayed up almost the whole night, sitting wakeful in the middle of my bed like a frog on a lily pad…. And at some time during these long hours I decided, hugging myself with determined delight, to make exactly what [artistic works] I wanted to make.[3]

How has a feeling of mystery been an aspect of your spirituality? ✍

LOVE

The holy may break in on our routine lives and suffuse us with love. An unexpected act of generosity may make us aware of how deeply someone cares for us. The steadfastness of friends, family, or support group members may carry us safely to the other side of a crisis. After a difficult conflict with a friend, when harmony has come again, we may feel a deep sense of mutual understanding beyond the merely human.

We may feel compassion emanating from a sacred source, a being or an energy beyond ourselves. When I am confused about something in my life, a dream often offers me a gentle suggestion as to how I might clarify it; when I am afraid to take a risk, a dream often reassures me. As we face the damage we may have done to ourselves and others, we may feel touched by a spirit of forgiveness.

Nelle Morton relates a love-filled encounter she had with the sacred while working with Betty, a twelve-year-old who had stopped speaking at age six:

> Together the children made a large puppet theater out of a refrigerator box; then each one made a puppet. One by one, they went into the stage/box/theater, put their fingers in the head and arms of the puppet and talked for [it].... Betty finished her puppet with help, put three fingers in the head, the thumb and little finger in the arms with help, then the children urged her to go into the stage. She did. She waved to the children with her free hand. They cried: "With the puppet!" She waved with the puppet, then leaned down near the puppet to hear the puppet speak. The puppet did not speak. Then she turned it toward her and looked it squarely in the face. Then she turned it back toward the children. "Speak! Speak!" they cried together. Suddenly she made the puppet bow toward Sidale and said, "Hi, Sidale!" Then she went around the room calling each by name. The children were ecstatic. I wept. All clapped their hands and rushed toward me: "Betty speak! Betty speak!" And Betty, laughing with them, said to me: "I speak! I speak!"[4]

How have you been touched by the sacred through the love of others? ✍

HARMONY AND CONNECTION

An encounter with the sacred may fill us with a profound sense of believing. We may feel at home in a special group of people. We may be in harmony with ourselves; we may feel unusually calm or quiet or in touch with our deepest inner wisdom. We may experience ourselves as an integral part of nature, not just an observer.

Alfred Painter, in an anthology about growing old, describes an experience of harmony and connection he had at age eighteen:

> I lived on Queen Anne Hill in Seattle. My favorite pastime was to climb to the park at the top of the hill to sit and watch the city below and the surrounding mountains to the west. One day at dusk, a particularly clear and unusually sunny day, I became entranced by the movement around me and my mind began to tune in to the complex, integrated mass of movement of the humans below me, all interconnected in various ways. I found myself caught up in it as part of my own being. I became aware of the red taillights on cars leaving the city as well as of the headlights of cars coming toward the city. I became aware of the many other forms of connectedness.... In my mind's eye I saw people from all over the world arriving in Seattle—and leaving it—and I personally felt this massive interconnectedness of life.... I became aware of the towers in the distance sending out radio waves connecting us to others around the globe. It occurred to me that the vast, sprawling city was really like a living organism with the coming and going of the people flowing like blood through the vessels of the planet—and I was an integral part of it.... The walls that separated me from the world dissolved and a great weight was lifted from my shoulders. Sensing the surge of life in everything around me, I knew, for the first time in my life, that I belonged in the world and that everything was as it should be.[5]

Make a note in your journal about your experiences of harmony and connection. ✍

WHOLENESS AND HEALTH

The word "holy" comes from the same root word as the words "whole" and "healthy." We may experience wholeness when a struggle of months or years suddenly comes to resolution or when we are able to accept, even welcome, a quality in ourselves we had previously rejected. For many gay men and lesbians, coming out is such an experience. People who lived in the shadow of shame find a self-acceptance that includes a sense of wholeness and health. As our relationship with the sacred deepens, we come to possess a new vitality and self-esteem. Our energy is more focused. We may feel less conflict and more peace within ourselves.

In the novel *Family Pictures*, by Sue Miller, the narrator confronts her mother about the pain of her childhood—especially the pain caused by an unresolved struggle in her parents' marriage. After a long conversation, they exchange apologies and she goes to bed.

> And then I went back to the guest room and shut the door, and fell nearly instantly into a heavy, befuddled sleep. But …I woke again, quite suddenly…. My mind was working frantically, running over the events of the evening, and I realized, staring at the shadowed medallion in the center of the ceiling, that I'd never heard [my mother] speak of *forgiving* or *not forgiving* my father before this night. That through all he'd done to her with his passionate belief… she'd never let on that she saw herself as injured or damaged by him. And even tonight…she hadn't spoken of that ancient, deep wound that had sat at the center of their marriage for so many years.
>
> It seemed to me that although my father was right in his wish for my mother to move on with him, she was right, too, to want to cling to the memory of that earlier time when she'd lived a life whose dimensions were so cramped by duty and love but also so spiritually expansive. Lying in the dim

light, I could see what they both wanted, and why. And I realized that I held them blameless for that. I had the peaceful sense of forgiving each of them on behalf of the other, as I drifted back to sleep.[6]

If you wish, make a note of any spiritual experiences you have had which involved a sense of wholeness and health. ✍

HEALING

Many of us become aware of the sacred through healing. Just as there are many ways of being wounded or broken—physically, emotionally, relationally—so too are there many ways of being healed. Healing touches places where we are still merely surviving and transforms us so we can truly come to life. It rewrites our personal story, replacing terror with trust and rage with serenity.

Sometimes we are mended in our relationships with others. This was the case for a friend of mine, who wrote this story:

Over a period of time one summer I gradually became more and more depressed, almost without realizing it. I had absolutely no energy. All I wanted to do was sleep. I couldn't think about anything but the most immediate, concrete things—like getting dressed, eating, sleeping. I didn't want to be around people and when I was I couldn't think of anything to say. I couldn't even feel desperate or sad. The only feeling I could feel was afraid. I knew that something was terribly wrong with me and I couldn't change it. I had never felt this way before.

During the worst part of my depression, I was on vacation with my partner. I was terrified that she would be angry with me, that she would criticize me and demand that I pull myself together. I was afraid she would leave me there and go home, because I was worse than a zombie to be with. So all the time I was trying to do everything I could to be cheerful

33

and energetic, but I couldn't. I couldn't do anything to change the way I felt.

Through the whole time of our vacation she never hurt me in any way. She accepted the fact that I was ill, and she seemed to know that I couldn't do any better than I was doing. She suggested things we could do each day, but if I didn't feel I could do them, she seemed to understand. She listened to me when I could get something into words, and she held me when I was afraid.

Ever since then I have felt safe in a way I never did before. This experience healed years and years of abuse.

At other times, healing seems to come directly from the divine to us. Nelle Morton, writing of a trip she took after she had retired, described how she was freed from a phobia she had had for many years:

Soon after my flight to New York had left the airport, the sky turned dark and we were caught in extremely turbulent weather. All my life I had been frightened of heights. I could not remember a time when I was at ease in the air—even in smooth skies.... In this particular storm...the thought came—what would happen if I invoked the Goddess!...I no sooner had such a thought than I leaned back in my seat and closed my eyes. Suddenly, it was as if someone had eased in the...seat next to me and placed her hand on my arm. "Relax," she said. "Let go of all your tightness. Feel your weight heavy against the seat and your feet heavy on the floor. The air has waves as does the ocean. You can't see them, but if you let yourself be carried by them you can feel their rhythm—even in turbulence. The pilot has been here before. He knows what he is doing. Even in the worst weather....Now breathe, breathe deeply. Ride the waves. Let yourself become a part of the rhythm."

I did as she directed. Fear left my muscles. I did indeed

34

feel the rhythm. Soon, I was enjoying the ride.... I was unafraid. Nor have I been afraid in a plane since that day.[7]

Have you had spiritual experiences which involved healing? ✍

HEIGHTENED AWARENESS AND CONCENTRATION

Some experiences of the sacred result in heightened awareness and concentration. We may be with a friend who suddenly switches from talking about superficial things to revealing her struggle to discern her sexual orientation. At such moments, we may become focused, more concentrated, more able to bring ourselves to the conversation. While bird-watching or deer hunting, we may, in the required stillness, find our senses to be unusually sharp and our concentration exceptionally acute.

Nelle Morton describes a meeting of a women's group in which this kind of intense, focused connection among the women allowed the woman speaking to connect fully with herself:

> The last day of the workshop the woman...wandered off alone. As we gathered sometime later in small groups she started to talk in a hesitant, almost awkward manner. "I hurt," she began. "I hurt all over." She touched herself in various places before she added, "But I don't know where to begin to cry. I don't know how to cry." Hesitatingly she began to talk. Then she talked more and more. Her story took on fantastic coherence. When she reached a point of the most excruciating pain, no one moved. No one interrupted her. No one rushed to comfort her. No one cut her experience short. We simply sat. We sat in a powerful silence. The women...went with her to the deepest part of her life.... The woman finished speaking. Tears flowed from her eyes.... She spoke again: "You heard me. You heard me all the way.... *You heard me to my own story. You heard me to my own speech.*"[8]

How have you experienced the sacred through heightened awareness and concentration? ✍

MAJESTY

An encounter with the sacred may alert us to the majesty of our sur-roundings. I remember hiking a path up a deep, narrow, dark canyon in Arizona. Suddenly, I found myself at the top of a ridge, from which I could see for many miles in all directions—miles and miles of sandstone formations, canyons, and desert. Far in the distance were blue mountains with snow-covered summits. I felt both exhilarated and humbled by the sight of this vast wilderness.

How has the sacred touched you through experiences of majesty? ✍

ENERGY

Encounters with the sacred often are charged with divine energy. Sometimes our own energy is inexplicably increased and we feel unusu-ally lively. For some of us, running, biking, or swimming can seem like holy events because they stimulate this sense of reanimation. Sometimes a time of laughter, play, or lovemaking can bring out the energetic dimen-sion of the sacred.

In other experiences, we may be directed by energy from outside our-selves or from a place deep inside that we do not control. We may feel called to change some aspect of our lives, to take a risk, to try a new approach to a frustrating situation. Conversion experiences are the most powerful encounters with the energy of the divine, but less intense encounters are actually fairly common in everyday life.

Not long ago the worship committee at my church asked me and three other members of the congregation to briefly tell a story of a time we had felt in exile. Our stories replaced the sermon that Sunday. Just before it was my turn to speak, I became very nervous because the story I was about to tell was a painful one and I wasn't sure I could get through it. My mouth was dry and my heart was racing. I closed my eyes and focused on my breathing, trying to calm down. As I did, I heard a voice inside saying, *Peg, you need to tell this story and some people in this room need to hear it. Remember: you're safe here.* A deep calm seemed to come over me, and I was able to tell my story without even looking at my notes.

Another way we may encounter the energy of the sacred is through what Carl Jung called synchronicity. We experience synchronicity in seemingly chance events that lead us in a particular direction or solve a problem for us.

Frederick Buechner, in his book *Telling Secrets*, describes an incident that occurred when he was grappling with his daughter's life-threatening eating disorder:

> I remember sitting parked by the roadside once, terribly depressed and afraid about my daughter's illness and what was going on in our family, when out of nowhere a car came along down the highway with a license plate that bore on it the one word out of all the words in the dictionary that I needed most to see exactly then. The word was TRUST.[9]

Have you encountered the sacred in any of these kinds of energy? If so, make a brief note in your journal. ✍

LONGING OR HUNGER

In mid-life, many people find that all they have acquired and achieved goes stale and that they are longing in a primal way for something they cannot put into words. They wonder, Is this all there is? Because such longing is focused on something beyond ourselves, I think of it as a spiritual experience. Harry Lee Shaw, a recovering alcoholic, describes a turning point in his life when he had twenty years' sobriety:

> But as I grew in sobriety and found my temporal life taking on new and vivified meaning, I began to feel that I was missing

spiritual growth and dedication. I missed, and missed poignantly, the faith, the firm belief in God which I had had as a child and as a young man.[10]

Others of us may feel driven or compelled at times by an inexplicable, primal hunger for the sacred. Such a feeling can surface at the beginning of our spiritual journey or after we have been traveling for some time. Indeed, it can become the central focus of our lives for months or even years.

Still others of us, such as the client who started me on the professional part of my own spiritual journey, understand intuitively that our recovery cannot unfold beyond a certain point without a personal, inner understanding of spirituality. The hunger we experience may be for a more stable or joyful way of life.

How have you known the sacred through longing or hunger? ✍

INEXPRESSIBILITY

When we meet the holy, we usually know it. We may feel shaken or encouraged, frightened or calmed, inspired or chastened, loved or insignificant. However, because spiritual experiences involve the whole of us and the unfathomable depth and unimaginable breadth of the holy, we cannot fully capture them in words.

In *Nine-Headed Dragon River*, Peter Mathiessen writes of one such experience:

> I lower my gaze from the snow peaks to the glistening thorns, the snow patches, the lichens. Although I am blind to it, the Truth is near, in the reality of what I sit on—rocks. These hard rocks instruct my bones in what my brain could never grasp in the *Heart Sutra* [an ancient sacred Buddhist text]....
>
> The secret of the mountains is that the mountains simply exist, as I do myself: the mountains exist simply, which I do not. The mountains have no "meaning," they *are* mean-

ing; the mountains *are*. The sun is round. I ring with life, and
the mountains ring, and when I can hear it, there is ringing
that we share. I understand all this, not in my mind but in
my heart, knowing how meaningless it is to try to capture
what cannot be expressed, knowing that mere words will
remain when I read it all again, another day.[11]

Have you had spiritual experiences which were impossible to describe in
words? ✍

At this point, I hope you are in touch with at least one personal spiritual
experience. Take a few minutes to review notes you made in your journal.
Mark the experiences you would like to explore in depth. It's useful to
note why you chose these particular memories.

If you are confused or you can't remember any spiritual experiences,
you could try taking a break for a few days. When we stop "trying" and
remain open, we often find what we need. Or you could continue with
another chapter. Memories are related to each other in surprising, non-
logical ways, and you may find that reading on will elicit memories of
spiritual experiences or open you to new ones.

Let yourself know if this is a good time to continue exploring your
sacred encounters. But give yourself the option of waiting until you are
ready.

PASSAGEWAY

Find a comfortable place to sit for about twenty minutes. Let your body
relax. Take a few deep breaths and begin the Passageway.

Imagine yourself as a tree growing in a sunny place. Let yourself see
the kind of tree you are. ❦ Do you have needles or leaves? ❦ Are you
big or small? ❦ Where are you growing? ❦ Let yourself become this
tree. ❦ Take a few minutes to become still, and let yourself feel the
life in the tree. ❦

When you're ready, gently turn your attention to your roots. ❧ Feel them anchored in the earth, holding you securely. ❧ Feel their strength. ❧ Now let yourself feel water and nutrients from the earth flowing up through your roots. ❧ Feel them flowing up, up, up into your trunk and out into your branches. ❧ Let every part of you experience this life-giving sap flowing through you. Breathe in and out, letting the feeling of fullness nourish you. ❧

Now turn your attention to your trunk. ❧ Feel its straightness. ❧ Let yourself feel its sturdiness, ring after ring. ❧ Begin at the core and move outward, through all the rings, until you feel your bark. ❧ Let yourself feel its toughness, protecting you from injury. ❧ Take a few minutes to experience your trunk, to feel its life and its strength. ❧

Now turn your attention to your branches and leaves or needles. ❧ Feel them reaching up and out. ❧ Feel the sun on your branches, feeding you from above, giving you what you need to grow. ❧ Notice how your leaves or needles reach toward the sun's light. ❧ Feel the warmth. ❧

Feel the breeze in your branches. ❧ Notice how supple they are, how they can bend without breaking. ❧ Let yourself experience the reach and arch of your branches. ❧

Now turn your attention to yourself as a whole. ❧ Be aware of your roots, trunk, and branches. ❧ Feel the flow of aliveness within, as you take in energy and let out what is no longer needed. ❧ Allow your breathing to become regular and deep as you experience your-self as a rooted, growing being. ❧ Stay with your breath for a few minutes, breathing in ❧ and out, ❧ in ❧ and out ❧ in and out, ❧ in and out. ❧

When you're ready, gently return to the present. Take a few min-utes to reorient yourself.

Now you could journal about your Passageway experience or go to the next section. Just sit quietly and let yourself know what would be best for you. ✍

EXPLORATION AND DISCOVERY

Now we'll look at some spiritual and religious experiences in depth. The goal is to immerse yourself in the memory so you can explore it from your current point of view.

Feeling safe is essential to spiritual exploration. If at any time you find you are overwhelmed with emotion—or you have "left" psychologically, consider stepping back from your exploration. Take a break until you regain your balance. Then select a less painful memory. You have the right to protect yourself from being retraumatized.

You may have jotted down memories that have little significance or feeling for you. Because they lack depth, they may not be fruitful choices for this exercise.

Now look over the experiences you marked for further exploration. Decide which one you will explore first. Allow about an hour for this exercise.

As you do the following exercise, remember to return to the Passageway exercise any time you need to become more quiet or focused.

You may want to alter the steps to make the exercise work best for you. Add information important to you but not specified in this exercise. Feel free to skip steps if they are not useful.

When you're ready, begin.

1. *Recenter yourself,* if necessary, by repeating some or all of the Passageway. Take time to become quiet and reflective.

2. *Tell the story of your experience* in detail. You may make a drawing or write about it. Use these questions as guides: ✍

   • Where and when did this happen? What time of year was it? How old were you? Was it during the day or night? Describe the

41

place and time in as much detail as you can.

- What happened? What was the sequence of events? Who was present during each part of the event? Give all the details you can remember. Include sensory data: What did you see, hear, taste, smell, touch? What did you feel in your body? Describe your emotional reactions. What feelings did you have at the time? Be as specific as you can.

Now look over your description or drawing to see whether you want to add to it. Notice your feelings during this review.

3. *Recenter yourself.* Are you still in a reflective, quiet space? If you find you're not focused or "in your head," return to the Passageway exercise for a few minutes, or close your eyes and rest for a short time.

4. *Reflect on the experience.* Sit quietly with the memory for a few moments. Let your mind range freely around the memory. What parts seemed especially important or charged with emotion? How did you feel about yourself and others? Have you had other similar experiences? Now write about your reflections. You can write any way you like. No grammar rules apply! ✎

5. *Name this experience* as if it were a book or movie. ✎

Since comparing several experiences can reveal themes in your relationship with the sacred, it can be illuminating to repeat this for a few more spiritual memories. If you prefer, take a break.

REFLECTION AND INTEGRATION

You just spent time immersing yourself in your encounters with the sacred. Now stand back and take a broader view. Take time to read over what you've written in your journal.

When you're ready, look over the following questions, which may guide you in finding patterns and themes in your spiritual experiences. Notice which questions appeal to you and which ones you would prefer to avoid.

- What do these memories tell me about my relationship with the sacred?
- What is the predominant tone of these experiences?
- Is there a place they all have in common? Indoors, outdoors, at home, in a place of worship?
- Was I alone or with others in these memories?
- What have I discovered about myself so far?
- Has anything surprised me?
- Has anything made me curious? Is there anything I want to know more about?

Now try asking yourself these questions. Listen for answers and write about them in your journal. Be as spontaneous as you can. ✍

You might want to take a break for a few days, weeks, or even months so you can integrate the discoveries about yourself as a spiritual person. Give yourself all the time you need to reflect, talk, or journal about your spiritual experiences and to experiment with what you have learned—before you go any further. New awarenesses are like seeds—they need time in stillness and darkness to germinate.

REFERENCES

1. Richard Solly, *Sacred Moments: Experiences of the Transcendent in the Lives of Ordinary Men* (to be published by Hazelden, 1995).
2. Frederick Buechner, *The Sacred Journey* (San Francisco, CA: Harper & Row, 1982), 2-3.
3. Anne Truitt, *Daybook, The Journal of an Artist* (New York: Pantheon, 1982), 150-51.
4. Nelle Morton, *The Journey Is Home* (Boston, MA: Beacon Press, 1985), 208.

5. Alfred Painter, "Reflection on the Isness," in *The Courage to Grow Old*, ed. Phillip L. Berman (New York: Ballantine Books, 1989), 1225-26.
6. Sue Miller, *Family Pictures* (New York: Harper & Row, 1990), 368-69.
7. Morton, 157-58.
8. Morton, 204-5.
9. Frederick Buechner, *Telling Secrets* (New York: Harper & Row, 1991), 49.
10. Harry Lee Shaw, "A Total Commitment," in *The Courage to Grow Old*, ed. Phillip L. Berman (New York: Ballantine Books, 1989), 239.
11. Peter Matthiessen, *Nine-Headed Dragon River* (Boston, MA: Shambhala Press, 1985), 95.

3.

RELIGION:

THE IMPERFECT INTERPRETER

Religion is a candle inside a multicolored lantern. Everyone looks through a particular color, but the candle is always there.
                                                    —Mohammed Naguib

Our religious background has a powerful effect on our adult spiritual life. Religion can be defined as *the human institution that carries spiritual traditions and practices across time and space.* The purpose of religion is to foster, nourish, and sustain the life of the spirit. Yet, because it is a human institution, religion does this imperfectly. For many of us, this imperfection proved so painful or confusing that we adamantly rejected religion, and now we steadfastly steer away from any "religious" spiritual path.

We can't escape religion completely, though, for it is woven into the fabric of American culture. Almost everyone once recited the Pledge of Allegiance at school. We all experience Christmas and Easter through our culture. We've all seen artists' images of Jesus. We have heard religious music. We attend weddings and funerals in churches or temples. We know members of the clergy or religious orders.

In her memoir *An American Childhood*, Annie Dillard, whose family was Protestant, describes her fright at seeing nuns when she was a young child:

> One afternoon…I was sitting stilled on the side-yard swing…
>
> St. Bede's was, as the expression had it, letting out; Jo Ann Sheehy would walk by again, and all the other Catholic children, and perhaps the nuns. I kept an eye out for the nuns….
>
> In the leafy distance up Edgerton I could see a black phalanx. It blocked the sidewalk; it rolled footlessly forward like a tank. The nuns were coming. They had no bodies, and imitation faces. I quitted the swing and banged through the back door and ran in to Mother in the kitchen.[1]

Usually our primary link to religion is through our family, where it is mixed with ethnic, racial, and regional traditions. People with formal religious backgrounds know about religious communities, clergy members, rituals, sacraments, and doctrines.

At home, religion may have been part of your family's lifestyle. You may have said grace before meals, prayed the rosary, or prayed at bedtime. Your parents may have read from sacred scripture or gone to Sabbath services. You may have heard your parents talking—or arguing—about religion.

What was religion like in your childhood community? Did you sing in the choir or attend church socials, catechism, or Hebrew classes? Did you go to Sunday school or other worship services? Were you taught religious stories? Did you memorize scripture passages? If your family was Christian, were you confirmed? If you were Jewish, did you have a bar or bat mitzvah?

We may have learned that persons of other religious traditions were misguided or inferior, or we may have been taught that respect should be shown to persons of all traditions. One woman described how her parents managed their families' religious differences.

My father was a Roman Catholic of Irish descent and my mother was a Missouri Synod Lutheran. In the forties and fifties, when I was growing up, those were two faiths that did not really have a lot to say to each other. Because it was a "mixed marriage," they could not have a church wedding and had to be married in the rectory.

My parents and their extended families developed an elaborate protocol as to how they would handle the differences. My dad said there was no reason to make a show of our religion, so we did not have statues, holy pictures, or crucifixes in our house. When my mother's large family came to dinner, as they frequently did, Dad instructed us, "Now don't make a big production of crossing yourselves at meal prayers." When we went to her relatives' homes for a meal on Friday, they usually did not serve meat. But if they forgot and served it, we had orders from Dad to eat it and not say a word.

In the Catholic church we were taught that when we attended weddings or funerals in other churches we were not to participate. "Nuts to that," said mother. "When they stand, you stand; when they sit, you sit. And at least try to sing the hymns."[2]

Some of us had devastating encounters with clergy from our family church or synagogue that made us wary of religion for decades. Gary Phelps, a gay man who tells his story in *The Search for Meaning*, describes his experience:

The first person I told I was gay was Father Leo, a Catholic priest who worked at the summer Boy Scout camp I attended in high school....He said, "Why are you telling me this? It's disgusting. I don't want to hear about it." I said that I was praying to change; that I prayed every day....

I asked for penance, but Father Leo said that I couldn't have it; I wasn't forgiven because I chose to be a sinner. He said, "You served at my Mass earlier this week." He started yelling, saying that I was the devil incarnate and that because of me Christ was never on the altar...that whenever I was present...everything was null and void....I ran into the woods and I stayed out overnight. I got lost, and I couldn't remember when I came back what had happened.[3]

We are triply wounded when clergy abuse us: in our relationship with ourselves, our religious community, and our God.

We might have been raised in a family that was clearly antireligion or antichurch. The adults might have talked disparagingly about religion or devout people. As a result, we may have felt odd or different from others or left out of community activities. Maybe we felt our inner questioning and curiosity about religion were wrong, silly, or abnormal.

Make a few notes, if you wish, about your family's relationship with religion. ✍

Whatever our religious heritage, we sift it through our own temperament, values, fears, struggles, and reactions. For example, we may have been touched by certain scripture passages, frightened by others, turned off by still others. Maybe we admired or idolized clergy members. Possibly they bored or scared us.

An orthodox Jewish man relates this story of how he was deeply touched by a simple gesture in the synagogue.

At the age of thirteen I remember davening one day and seeing the rabbi bow, and it was a very divine moment for me. Because the thought that he bows to something...or someone...was awesome. And his bowing was so simple, so unassuming, so innocent, so natural that it wasn't like he was being religious when he bowed or that he was being pious. It was like he was transparent, and whatever he was bowing to suddenly became very important.[4]

An excerpt from Annie Dillard's *An American Childhood* captures an angry and disillusioned adolescent's view of a Sunday service:

> Nothing so inevitably blackened my heart as an obligatory Sunday at the Shadyside Presbyterian Church...the minister's Britishy accent; the putative hypocrisy of my parents, who forced me to go, though they did not; the putative hypocrisy of the expensive men and women who did go....
>
> After the responsive reading there was a pause, an expectant hush. It was the first Sunday of the month, I remembered, shocked. Today was Communion. I would have to sit through Communion, with its two species, embarrassment and tedium—I would be late getting out and Father would have to drive around the block a hundred times. I had successfully avoided Communion for years.[5]

What religious events had emotional significance (positive or negative) when you were a child? ✍

Some of us attended church-affiliated schools. Our experiences there may have deepened wounds we had already received, or helped us heal. One woman remembered her experience at a Catholic school:

> I stayed after school a lot in the third grade. Sister Beatrice Ann "invited" me to practice my handwriting on the blackboard, an illogical consequence for talking in class and disturbing others. I would receive the same invitation if my papers were sloppy. Many late afternoons I walked with Sister to the convent across the street after we locked the classroom.
>
> Quite often Sister gave me an apple or other treat a student might have brought her. Sometimes I was invited into the convent for cookies or to take home clothes someone had donated for poor students.
>
> Gradually I came to understand that Sister Beatrice Ann

took me under her care in a way that wouldn't appear to be favoritism. My time after school with her was nurturing. She made me feel special at a time in my life when I needed this attention.

If you attended a religious school, write down the memories that seem significant. ✍

When we got older, we might have looked to other faiths. Perhaps we attended services or read scriptures from other spiritual traditions, comparing them with ours. And we all know people with different beliefs from our own.

If you explored any other religious traditions, take a moment to note any memories that come to mind. ✍

You might have had deeply moving spiritual experiences when you took part in religious activities. Maybe it was when you received communion or heard scripture readings.

In this excerpt from her journal, Ellen Anthony described an experience in a religious setting, and it was clearly spiritual for her:

> One day in Meeting for Worship Charlotte stood up and recited Psalm 139. When she got to "Thou has beset me behind and before, and laid thine hand upon me," I dissolved. Tears just came and I realized I was in, not out. God in front of me, behind me, and the Big Hand on me. It is so strange how that can happen: I was always outside of whatever love or world or happiness I saw and then I was inside it and there was no outside.[6]

Make a note of any experiences you have had which are both religious and spiritual. ✍

I hope these examples have put you in touch with some of your religious experiences. If not, it could be beneficial to take a break for a few days to talk with your family about religious events in your childhood. Give yourself whatever time you need to remember more about your religious history.

Now look over the religious experiences you have listed. Choose two or three you'd like to explore more deeply. Mark them in some way so you can easily find them later.

PASSAGEWAY

This exercise requires you to pause frequently. It should take about twenty-five minutes. Find a comfortable place to sit, and when you are ready, begin.

Let your body settle into the chair, bench, or floor. ❦ Be aware of the body parts you are holding up, beginning with your facial muscles. ❦ Gently let go of the muscles of your face ❦ the muscles in your forehead ❦ around your eyes ❦ around your mouth. ❦ Let your face become soft and relaxed. ❦

Now bring your attention to the back of your head and your neck. Be aware of any tension there ❦ any energy beyond what you need to hold up your head. ❦ Gently let go of that extra stress ❦ Let the muscles come to a place of balance ❦ a place where they can do their job without straining. ❦ Feel them soften and relax. ❦

Bring your awareness to your shoulder muscles and your upper back. ❦ Notice any tautness there ❦ and how it feels. ❦ Now let your shoulders hang loosely. ❦ Let them drop into a position where they are soft ❦ and at rest. ❦

Notice any taut muscles in your back or lower parts of your body. ❦ Let them slacken, a little at a time. ❦ Let them soften. ❦ Notice how they are still holding you up, even though they are relaxed and at rest. ✹

Take a few minutes now to enjoy this state of calm and relaxation. ✹ Just be with yourself for a few minutes. ✹ A time with no demands ✹ no hurry ✹ nothing to accomplish ✹ nowhere to rush off to ✹ a time just to be ✹ just to live.

When you are ready, slowly and gently return to the present. Take your time making the transition. Stretch a bit. ✍

If your sense of calm should fade as you do the exercises in the following sections, give yourself a little time to reconnect with the Passageway.

When you wish, go on to the Exploration and Discovery section.

EXPLORATION AND DISCOVERY

For some of us, religious experiences are intertwined with emotional, physical, or sexual abuse. Choose your memories with a spirit of love and concern for yourself and your emotional well-being. If you become flooded with emotion or psychologically absent as you do the exercise, take a break to restore your equilibrium before you go further.

Remember that the steps of the exercise are just suggestions. If some do not fit for you, feel free to skip them. It may be useful to write about what makes them abrasive or foreign to you. Change the exercise to whatever is most beneficial for you. If you are pulled in a direction apparently unrelated to the exercise, follow that thread for a while. You may discover something of great importance.

Give yourself about an hour to complete the first part of the exercise. If you plan to finish this chapter, you will probably need about two hours.

Now look back over the religious experiences you marked earlier. Choose one and follow these steps:

1. *Do the Passageway* exercise from this or some other chapter.

2. *Tell the story of the experience* from your point of view. Include all the details you can remember. You may use the following questions as a guide, but do not let them limit you: ✍

   • Where and when did this experience take place? What time of year was it? How old were you? Did it happen during the day or at night? Describe the place and time with as much detail as possible.

   • What happened? What was the sequence of events? Who was present at each step in the event? What did you see, hear, taste, smell, or touch? What did you feel in your body? Also include your emotional response to the experience. What feelings did you have as this event took place? Be as specific as you can.

Now that you have described the experience, look it over as a whole. If you want to add other details, do so now. Jot down any feelings you have. ✍

3. *Recenter yourself.* Notice whether you are still in a reflective, quiet space. If you are tired or unfocused, return to the Passageway exercise or take time to rest and relax.

4. *Reflect on the experience.* Sit quietly with the memory. Let your mind wander around the experience. Be aware of the parts that are particularly charged with emotion or meaning. How do you feel about yourself in the memory? Have you had other similar experiences? ✍

5. *Name the experience* as if it were a book or movie. ✍

This is a good place to take a break, if you wish. You could repeat this process for other religious memories.

REFLECTION AND INTEGRATION

In this chapter, you've explored one religious experience in depth and probably remembered several others. Now it's time to take an eagle-eye view—to see how your experiences are alike or different, connected or separate.

When you're ready, use a Passageway exercise or another method you like to get quiet and focused.

Now review what you wrote in the last section. Can you discern common threads in your religious experiences?

- Does one feeling pervade all my religious experiences?
- Is there a place or a kind of place common to all of them?
- Are they primarily solitary or communal?
- What have I discovered about myself in this chapter?
- Has anything surprised me?
- Has anything made me curious? Do I want to know more about anything?

As you sit quietly, you may find that patterns and truths appear in a fragmented, nonlinear way. It's okay to write just that way. Write a few words, cross them out if they don't seem right, even grope for words. Feel free to ignore the lines, write sideways, scribble, or draw if you want. Let your spirit speak in whatever voice fits. ✍

In reflecting on what you've learned about yourself, you may be thinking about what comes next. Is there anything you'd like to experiment with? Pursue? Is there a subject you want to explore over a longer time? ✍

You might enjoy talking about your new awareness with a partner, friend, therapist, or support group. Think about the people you trust and feel safe with. Are there parts of your story you would share with them? Are there parts you aren't ready to talk about? ✍

You might need more time or privacy to reflect. In your journal note anything about time and privacy that is important to your present spiritual

exploration. Whatever your situation, you can do what fits best for you.
✍

This might be a good place to break. You have new awarenesses to mull over, integrate, and experiment with in your daily life. You may want to do more writing, talking, or drawing to explore your experiences more deeply. Let yourself know what you need for now.

REFERENCES
1. Annie Dillard, *An American Childhood* (New York: Harper & Row, 1987), 33-34.
2. Mary Bednarowski, professor, United Theological Seminary, in an informal lecture at St. Mary's Graduate Center, Minneapolis, 1988.
3. Gary Phelps, "Jim Bob," in *Search for Meaning: Americans Talk About What They Believe*, ed. Phillip L. Berman (New York: Ballantine Books, 1990), 41-42.
4. Chabad Hasid, (untitled), *Search for Meaning*, 381.
5. Annie Dillard, 196.
6. Ellen Anthony, "Somebody Has to Die," *Weavings* (May-June 1991): 29.

4.

PIECES FROM THE PAST:
A FRESH PERSPECTIVE

Life for me is a profound, a sacred, a joyous,
a mysterious, a soulful dance.

—*Anaïs Nin*

*E*very year I visit the quilt display at the fair. Of the scores of quilts
there, many have traditional patterns—the star, the wedding ring,
the log cabin. Others have a contemporary design or tell a story. Some
are simple, some elaborate. Each uses color and shape to create a mood
all its own. Some show the skill of experienced quilters, while others are
the first fruits of beginners.

Quilts are made with dozens of bits of fabric sewn together to create
a whole that pleases both eye and spirit as no one piece could. Like a
quilt, every human life is unique, every pattern and color motif different.

Sometimes we can't see our own life patterns and colors clearly. We
live life day to day, our energy invested in the details of family, work, and
recreation. Seldom do we have the time to step back and see the larger
view that would tell us where we've been and where we seem to be going
on our spiritual path.

If we learned to hide our true feelings to survive difficult childhood experiences, we come to our journey without a good idea of who we are. If we were to make quilts of our lives, some of the pieces would be missing, others might be distorted.

When our emotional or physical survival is threatened, whether we are children or adults, we don't have much energy for objective observation. Most of our attention is focused on anticipating and avoiding more wounds, or healing from the old ones. We see only certain parts of our history and inner lives, and we give some of them more importance than they deserve. If we are survivors of child abuse, we may feel responsible for it. We may overemphasize our "bad" qualities while completely overlooking our good ones. Because of our pain, we may even forget or minimize the lively, successful, loving, or inspiring parts of ourselves or our story.

No matter what has cut us off from awareness of the patterns and colors of our lives, when we begin to grow spiritually we seek greater self-awareness and self-knowledge. We try to learn all we can about what connects us with the sacred and what cuts us off from it.

You have already begun to gather pieces for your life quilt—the pieces relating to your spiritual and religious experiences. In this chapter, you will add more pieces and assemble them in order to see how they are related and what they tell you about your past and your future. As you do, you will begin to see the patterns that have been hidden or camouflaged in daily routines.

PASSAGEWAY

Before you do this exercise, gather some big sheets of paper (11" x 17" is good) and some colored pens or pencils. (A multicolored set of eight or ten fine-point marking pens will do fine.) Bring your journal too, because you may want to write. When you're ready, begin.

Bring your attention gently to your breath. Notice how you're breathing right now, without trying to change it. ❧ Notice how your breath feels as it moves through your nose ❧ in and out ❧ in and out. If your mind wanders, gently bring it back to awareness of your breathing. Breathe in and out in out Continue to focus on your breathing for a few minutes.

Now imagine that you are sitting with a quilter who is sewing a bed-size quilt. Picture the quilter now. Is this someone you know or someone new? Is the quilter male or female? How old is the quilter? Imagine what his or her face looks like. What is the color of this person's eyes? Hair? Skin? How is the quilter dressed? Be aware of as many details as you can about this person. What do you sense about the quilter? What does your intuition tell you? Picture your surroundings. What can you see? Notice the season and the time of day. Be aware of any sounds you hear.

Take a little time to simply be with the quilter. Notice any feelings you have.

The quilter is making a quilt that represents your life. Look at the quilt. Take the time to observe it in detail. Is it heavy or light? What colors has the quilter chosen? Do they blend together or stand in sharp contrast? Are they solid or patterned? Be aware of how you feel about the colors. What are the textures of the various pieces? Now touch them and feel their textures. Notice the shapes of the various pieces. Are they small or large? Take the time to notice each piece of the quilt and notice how you feel as you do.

Now notice the whole quilt. Can you see what the pattern will be? Perhaps it is a patchwork or abstract design, a circle, a star, or a set of squares. Is it bold or subtle? What feelings do you have about the pattern?

Take as much time as you want to experience the quilter, the quilt, and yourself. Be aware of all details and feelings.

When you are ready, return your attention to your breathing. Notice your breath moving in and out 🍃 in and out 🍃 by itself. 🍃 Stay with this awareness for a few minutes, noticing when you breathe in 🍃 and when you breathe out. 🍃 Feel the air going in 🍃 and out of your body. 🍃

Now gently bring your attention back to your surroundings. 🍃 Take plenty of time for the transition. 🍃 There is no need to hurry. 🍃 Just gently bring yourself back.

If you wish, make a brief note of how you have experienced this Passageway. ✎

EXPLORATION AND DISCOVERY

In this section, you will draw a line to represent your life and then place significant life events, spiritual events, and religious events on it. As you work on your lifeline, at times you will probably be surprised by what you remember. Buried feelings may surface. You may be moved or upset. Take time to be present to whatever arises. Allow yourself to grieve, to rejoice, to savor, to be angry, as you reflect on your life as a whole. If you start to feel overwhelmed or numb, give yourself permission to take a break and come back to the exercise later.

As you place events on your lifeline, remember that this is just *one* look at your life. If you were to repeat the exercise months or years from now, you would probably add events. Others would seem less important than they do now. As we mature, we constantly revise our view of our history, so there is no need to try to be complete or exact. Let yourself know what seems most important today, and that will be enough.

Sometimes we hesitate to claim the importance of an event because we don't understand why it had such an impact on us. I encourage you to trust your inner sense that something is or was pivotal in your life even if you can't explain why.

As you go ahead with the exercise, remember that significant events

60

may be positive or negative, happy or painful. Usually what makes them important is that they have changed us. Keep in mind that you're the one who knows best what is or isn't important.

This exercise works best if you read all the directions first. If you decide to do the exercise in one sitting, allow about an hour and a half.

1. Draw Your Lifeline

First, choose either a color to represent your whole life or several colors to represent different periods of your life. It may be useful to note why you picked the colors you did. Now you're going to represent your life by drawing a line across the middle of your paper. After you draw the line, make points along it to represent your age. It could be a horizontal "scale" marked with five- or ten-year increments, for example.

2. Place Significant Life Events Along Your Lifeline

First center yourself until you feel focused and relaxed by using the Passageway exercise or any other method you prefer.

Now choose a color and write important events in your life along the line at the age you were when they happened. Identify them with only a word or two. (You will place specific religious and spiritual events on your lifeline later, but you may include them now if you wish.) You may easily recall events, or they may come to you slowly. Trust your own process, and take all the time you need to complete this step. When you finish, sit quietly for a time to see if anything else surfaces.

If nothing more seems to come to you, stretch a bit or make a cup of tea. When you return, look over the events you have placed on the line. Do you see common threads? Do they fall into specific time periods? Are they similar or very different? If you see any patterns, note them on your lifeline sheet or in your journal. ✍

3. Place Significant Spiritual Events on Your Lifeline

Now relax and recenter yourself. When you're ready, choose a color to represent significant *spiritual* events. If you wish, place on the line any or all events you identified in chapter 2. Add anything else that comes to you. If some of your life events are also spiritual, use both colors to note that.

When you reach a point where no more events are coming to you, sit quietly with your lifeline for a few minutes. Sometimes during a period of quiet, additional memories emerge.

When you are finished with this step, I encourage you to take a short break. When you return, take another look at your lifeline. Can you see any patterns or common threads in the events that touched you spiritually? Are there any inconsistencies in these experiences? Any consistencies? ✐

Now refresh your mind before you go on. Doing dishes, pulling weeds, and folding laundry provide good breaks for me.

4. PLACE RELIGIOUS EVENTS ON YOUR LIFELINE

Now choose a color for religious events and place them on the line. These may not be the ones your loved ones would identify! They may have had either a positive or a negative impact on you. You could use some of what you wrote in chapter 3. Feel free to sort through it. Also, add anything else you remember now.

Pause when you seem to be finished. Again, if nothing else emerges, take a break. Then look for patterns in your religious experiences. ✐

At this point an hour or two of rest might add richness to the remainder of the exercise. Later, you may find that your unconscious was still processing information while you were doing something else.

5. NOTICE THE RELATIONSHIPS BETWEEN ALL THE EVENTS

Now look at your lifeline again.

Focus on how your life, spiritual, and religious events are connected.

Patterns and conflicts you see will be uniquely your own. Here are typical conclusions people can draw from their lifelines:

- I had no spiritual life until I was sober.
- At my father's funeral, I saw right through religion and I haven't been back since.
- In the past ten years, my spiritual life has centered around my dreams.
- I was a very religious child until confirmation, but then I just quit religion. It seemed so phony to me.
- When I was a kid, my spiritual life was in the farm fields every day. Religion meant nothing to me.
- I have felt all my life that my religion and my spirituality were the same.
- When I was eleven years old, I stopped praying because I was mad at God for not making my mother stop drinking.
- I never had a spiritual experience until my first child was born.

Use your journal to describe the connections or relationships you've seen. Try to find the exact words to describe them. Ask yourself these questions to help you focus:

- Are religion and spirituality related or separate in my life?
- Are they harmonious or discordant?
- How do important times in my life connect to my spirituality or religion? Is there a cause-and-effect relationship? Does one seem to open the way for the other? Or does one block the path of the other? ✍

REFLECTION AND INTEGRATION

Think of your lifeline as a quilt that tells a story or evokes themes of your life. This quilt is uniquely yours. Though incomplete, it has had singular beauty and value from the beginning. Now you'll put what you've seen into words or pictures. Describing what's been true for you, even if only to yourself, makes it come alive. You're saying, This is important. I am important. What I want makes a difference.

Seeing ourselves as complex, multifaceted people can be hard work. It may be difficult to find words for some things you're learning about yourself. You may even be ashamed of some events on your lifeline.

It takes a lot of work to recover treasure at the bottom of the sea. That is what you might be doing in a way. Great effort may be necessary. Make sure you acknowledge your courage and effort. Treasure hunters give themselves time to rest and plan. After a dive, they return to the surface slowly to avoid the bends. They understand that without rest, they place themselves in danger. After you dive below the surface to recover lost inner connections, I hope you come up to rest.

Use the Passageway to center and quiet yourself. Then look at your lifeline from a distance. Hang it on a wall or set it on a table so you can see it as a whole. Do you have any feelings about it when you see it like this? ✍

Now look at your lifeline as if it were a map. See the sections as shapes rather than words. Try not to notice details yet. Let the spaces speak to you. What do the empty sections have to say? ✍

Look at the sections that are very full. What was true about those times in your life? ✍

Do you see anything else? ✍

Now sit back for a moment. Savor your discoveries before you move on.

When you're ready, look more closely at the lifeline. As you do, ask yourself some questions:

- What is the flow of events in my life? Which persons or events were sources of energy for change? Which ones blocked change?
- Which critical incidents were related to my spirituality? What was their impact?
- Are there definable periods of my history? How would I describe and name them? How did they begin and end? How would I

describe and name the period I am in now?
- What past challenges have I met in my spiritual life? How have I addressed them?
- What is my major challenge now? Which old events foster my present spiritual growth? Impede it?
- What did I discover about myself as a spiritual and religious person by doing my lifeline?
- What has surprised me?
- Is there anything on my lifeline I want to know more about?
- Is there anything else I can note?

Write about your reflections in a way that fits for you. Remember to let your writing match your inner voice. Write as much or as little as you wish. ✍

You have taken an in-depth look at your spiritual, religious, and life experiences. In the rest of the book, I will guide you while you learn how you have encountered major themes shared by all spiritual traditions: language, images of God and the sacred, prayer and meditation, community, ritual, and compassionate service.

5.

LISTENING FOR THE VOICE OF OUR SOUL

*Whatever can be truly expressed in its proper meaning must emerge
from inside a person and pass through an inner form. It cannot come
from outside to inside of a person, but must emerge from within.*
—*Meister Eckhart*

We need a new language that will draw us closer to the sacred, to
ourselves, and to others traveling a spiritual path. The language of
the soul speaks of wisdom beyond our usual knowledge. It connects the
most vulnerable part of us to the divine presence within and outside of us.

How do we recognize our soul's voice and language? When a hymn,
scripture reading, prayer, or ritual touches us deeply, it is our spirit both
listening and speaking. I was intensely moved several years ago when I
went to church after a long absence on a spring day, Palm Sunday. The
reading was about Jesus' triumphant entry into Jerusalem. In the story,
Jesus' followers are shouting out their joy. The Pharisees tell Jesus to quiet
them down, but Jesus replies, "I tell you, if they were to keep silence, even
the stones would shout out."[1] When this last sentence was read, a shiver
shot through my back and shoulders. Though I did not fully understand
what had happened inside me, I knew that Jesus' words had resonated
with some interior voice of my own.

We begin to hear our soul's voice when we are unexpectedly filled with joy and gratitude. Our feelings are the spirit's response to holiness in our lives. We also hear the voice of our spirit when a deep inner truth surfaces for us. This often comes after a long struggle during which solutions to our problems seemed limited. Maybe we've felt hopelessly victimized by people or circumstances. We've brooded over a problem, feeling trapped and getting nowhere. Unexpectedly, we are given a way out. Someone says something to free us, or we inadvertently stumble across a solution. Or we give up, exhausted, only to hear an inner voice tell us a basic, caring, and principled truth. This is the voice of our spirit.

We recognize the unique voice of our soul when we feel consonance with a specific religious expression or spiritual idea. For example, I was raised in the Christian tradition, but I feel a quiet harmony when I read the wisdom of the *Tao Te Ching*, written centuries ago by the Chinese sage Lao-tse. Many people have told me that although they were alienated from religion in childhood, they were—and continue to be—deeply moved by music of their family's religious tradition.

Our soul speaks to us when we feel guided by a wise presence either outside or inside us. A friend of mine shares this story:

> I went fishing way up in the mountains, far from a road. Many willows and bushes grew on both sides of the stream, with a rough path running through them. I was heading for the place where two streams come together. I walked and walked. I became somewhat afraid, thinking I should be there by now. Suddenly a voice—I couldn't tell if it came from inside or outside of me—said, "Just trust the path." Immediately, I felt calmer. I kept going, and I soon found the place where I wanted to fish. All day I thought about that message: Just trust the path. I thought how much it would simplify my life if I'd trust the path in other areas. I really got a lot out of that one sentence, wherever it came from.

How do you hear the voice of your soul? ✍

THE CHALLENGES OF LISTENING

To listen for our spirit, we need to move past the predictable, reflexive reactions we have—anger, fear, contempt, boredom—when we hear religious words and ideas. One man tells how difficult it is to hear anything from inside of him because of his intense angry reactions to anything connected to religious beliefs:

> It even bothers me in a bookstore. When I leaf through a book that looks interesting and see the words "God," "Jesus," or "Lord," I immediately close the book and put it back on the shelf. I feel like the author's laying his religious trip on me. It makes me angry.

We often mistake reactions like this for the voice of our spirit, but they're actually self-defense mechanisms. As we gently explore the complex beginnings of our defensiveness, we will hear the first faint sounds of our spirit. Are you aware of any knee-jerk reactions you have? ✍

We will need to discriminate between the voice of our soul and the voice of our intellect. The intellect defines, differentiates, argues, defends, analyzes, and critiques. It's easy to mistake an intellectual statement like "I do not believe in God" (or Jesus, or sin, or hell, or redemption) for a soul statement. In the past our intellect has often sustained us when something threatened to destroy our sense of ourselves. Clearly, intellect is vital to our survival, but it does not speak for our spirit. Do you have internal arguments about religion that masquerade as your true voice? ✍

We'll also need to distinguish between our voice and the voices of parents, relatives, teachers, and clergy in our past. Separating these voices from our own can be difficult, because we trusted them and depended on them when we were children. If we didn't develop a strong voice of our own, we may have to strain to hear it above the din of other voices we carry around with us. We may be surprised to remember other people's words involuntarily in moments of doubt or stress. Whose voice do you confuse with your own? What message is this voice giving you? ✍

We also need to distinguish our soul's voice from the voices of people we admire—ministers, teachers, therapists, spiritual leaders, writers, spiritual directors. This could be difficult, because these are voices we want to hear. The spiritual language of people we admire can help us clarify our own spiritual voice, but we have to remember that these voices are not our own. Whose voice resonates with yours? What messages bring out your own language of the spirit? ✍

As we follow a spiritual path, we choose to improve our conscious contact with the God of our understanding and the deepest parts of ourselves. We slowly, gently allow ourselves to explore what is behind our habitual responses and thoughts. Wherever our exploration leads, we gradually discover a living spirit within us, one with a unique language. Little by little we learn to recognize the voice of our soul, distinct from emotions, intellect, our parents' voices, religious traditions, teachers, clergy, and even opinions of our chosen spiritual guides. We become like a parent who can hear a child's cry over all the other sounds from a crowded playground. Make a few notes about how you recognize your spirit when it speaks. ✍

NEGATIVE CHILDHOOD EXPERIENCES OF RELIGION: POWERFUL SILENCERS OF OUR SPIRITUAL VOICE

The religious language we heard when we were children may have contributed to the silencing of our soul. At the very least, it probably restricted us to expressing selective ideas, traditions, images, and relationships. The expression of other ideas was implicitly or explicitly frowned upon. Catechism and strict religious education, for example, may define the imaginative ideas and questions from children about God as foolish or irreverent. Simple, rote answers may be given to profound questions about the nature of God. A man raised in a Catholic family in the 1940s remembers catechism on Saturday mornings when he was in elementary school:

The first picture I always get when someone talks about the

soul is one of milk bottles, because that was the way the soul was presented to me at a catechism class when I was in second grade. The priest had a picture of two milk bottles. One of them was completely black, and the other was peppered with thousands of little black dots. The one with the little dots was a soul with your normal, day-to-day venial sins, small sins. And the black one was your soul with a mortal sin. Here I am fifty-five years old, and when someone uses the word "soul," I see those milk bottles. One allows you to end up in heaven after many years in purgatory. With the other one, you get no chance of heaven.

Dogmatic teaching like this has a powerful effect on children. People whose religious background emphasized sin and damnation know how it created terror, especially if their families were dysfunctional in other ways.

For some people, the Bible reinforced physical abuse and punishment. Verses like "Spare the rod, spoil the child," a common phrase taken from a verse in Proverbs,[2] may have been used to rationalize physical punishment. Countless battering husbands have used the Bible verse "Wives, be subject to your husbands, as is fitting in the Lord"[3] to justify abuse. Bible passages are also used to fuel hatred of gay men and lesbians.[4] In each case, the verse is taken out of context, both historically and in relation to the rest of the story. Since as children (and often as adults) we don't have enough information to recognize this as misuse of the Bible, the abuse we suffered can seem to be linked to God.

People raised in dysfunctional families with no religious tradition may become estranged from the voice of their spirit because they feel alienated from what are usually considered "normal" beliefs and practices. One man, raised in a family that ridiculed religion and religious people, described his feelings when he was ten years old:

> I was walking alone across a baseball field, and suddenly I thought, *I don't believe in God.* I was aware that other people thought there was a God and believed in God. But I didn't. I

was clearly not experiencing what other people did. I had an incredibly empty, scary feeling, one that I now know to be shame. I just felt so bad about it. I was worried and pre-occupied with it for weeks. I was really scared.

How did your religious upbringing—or lack of it—stifle the voice of your spirit? ✍

THE SPIRITUAL CONSEQUENCES OF KEEPING THE SPIRIT SILENT

Whatever the specific cause, your spiritual growth may have slowed down or even stopped altogether. You could be limited to experiences, images, and language of your early childhood. It can be pretty difficult to believe God cares about you when you are terrified that God is watching for your mistakes.

As we begin to explore some ways to connect with the sacred, we may find that we have nothing to say—or that we have no God to say it to. We may feel so alienated that prayer is impossible. Our emotional chaos may make the inner quiet we need to pray practically impossible.

Talking with others allows us to reexamine our images of God and our ideas about prayer. A fresh look opens us to the possibility of a new relationship with the divine.

A carefully chosen spiritual community can be the catalyst for us to develop a prayer life. In community—whether in a Twelve Step program, church community, or an informal spirituality group—we can unite with other people to break the silence of our spirit. There we can find a safe, affirming, loving, and gentle environment where we can, at last, listen for the voice of our own soul.

Make a few notes, if you wish, about how silencing your spirit affected your spiritual life. ✍

WHEN LANGUAGE IS AN OBSTACLE TO WOMEN'S SPIRITUAL GROWTH

Through authentic and personally meaningful experiences, we begin to make a spiritual recovery, to know the sacred from the inside of ourselves.

In time we begin to speak—first to ourselves, and then to others. At this point, the patriarchal language of the Judeo-Christian tradition often becomes a problem for many women.

Some women are comfortable with the traditional masculine images and language, but many people—including men—are not.

Millions of women have struggled with the pronoun issue. Referring to God as "she" implies a humanlike God, which some people can't accept. "It" makes the God neuter, and few people, whether their image of God is humanlike or not, find this adequate. Addressing the sacred as God or Goddess solves the problem for some people, but many Christians and Jews reject this language because it clashes with the traditional scriptural language.

Most religious traditions don't provide leadership on the issue of patriarchal language. Some churches use *The Inclusive Language Lectionary*, but often only after a rancorous and divisive battle. The New Revised Standard Version of the Holy Bible, recently revised (again) after nearly four decades, deleted noninclusive language about human beings but retained masculine language about God. The same is true of other recent editions of the Bible.

You may need determination and courage to speak your own spiritual language despite the traditional patriarchal language you may encounter.

If you wish, make a few notes about how you have experienced this struggle. ✍

If we are women who were spiritually silenced by abuse and trauma, or by our often misogynistic and patriarchal culture, we can validate one other's frustration and anger. We can answer young people's questions about God differently than ours were answered. We can listen with respect to other people's spiritual experiences and grow beyond biases about appropriate pronouns. In these ways we honor and preserve one other's speech.

PASSAGEWAY

Take a few minutes to unwind. When you're ready, begin.

Become aware of what is happening within you at this moment. Gently bring your attention to your body. 🍃 How are you feeling physically? 🍃 Notice any parts of your body that are tense. 🍃 Allow them to relax. 🍃

Now be aware of how you're feeling emotionally. Notice any anxiety or agitation 🍃 any anger 🍃 any sadness. 🍃 Simply note where you feel them without trying to change them. 🍃 Notice any calmness or serenity you feel 🍃 any joy 🍃 any safety. 🍃 Be aware of where in your body you have these feelings without trying to hold onto them. 🍃 Just let them be. 🍃

Now bring your attention to your breath. 🍃 Breathe in 🍃 and breathe out. 🍃 Just notice the breath without trying to change it. 🍃 Breathe in and breathe out. 🍃 In 🍃 and out. 🍃

When you are ready, remember an experience when you were deeply heard as you expressed what was within you. Or create such an experience with your imagination. 🍃 Call to mind a person or group of persons who will listen carefully and lovingly to you. 🍃 Allow yourself to enter fully into this listening space. 🍃 Imagine the details of the setting and the person(s). 🍃 Let yourself experience the emotional climate of safety 🍃 of affirmation 🍃 of love 🍃 of gentleness. 🍃

Be aware of your physical self in this place. 🍃 How does your body feel? 🍃 Notice how you feel emotionally in a climate of listening. 🍃

If you find that you are distracted or absent, just gently bring yourself back to the image of a setting in which you can be truly heard 🍃 without criticism. 🍃 Just softly return to a safe 🍃 affirming 🍃 loving 🍃 gentle environment. 🍃

Allow yourself to enjoy this environment for a few minutes. 🍂 Just breathe in 🍂 and out 🍂 in this space. 🍂 Breathe in 🍂 and out 🍂 in this listening space. 🍂

When you're ready, gently bring yourself back to the present time and place. 🍂 Take whatever time you need. 🍂 Then take a few minutes to stretch and reorient yourself. 🍂

EXPLORATION AND DISCOVERY

These three exercises will heighten your awareness of the role of language in your spiritual life—the language that dampens it and the language that expresses it. Words, concepts, and images that have a negative connotation for us are sometimes more telling than those positive words which do not provoke as strong a response. The exercises will help you explore both.

As you do the exercises, free yourself from definitions and debates. Explore only the words that mean something to you. Hear the stories, see the images, and feel the emotions attached to the words.

You don't need to come to any decisions or conclusions about any of them. This is a time to expand your inner knowing, nothing more. Be open to as much as you can. If you begin to shut down, try to relax enough to explore a little further.

You will probably find that your unique spiritual language is muffled by layers of conventional, habitual, or reflexive responses. These easy, familiar associations are thoughts and feelings you've had for years. As you get closer to the sound of your own voice, you may be surprised. Your curiosity may grow. You may feel relief, or you could feel anger, joy, or grief. You might have a sense of newness. Reactions like these signal that you are beginning to hear your true spirit.

EXERCISE 1:

IDENTIFY YOUR PERSONAL RELIGIOUS

AND SPIRITUAL VOCABULARY

The list on pages 79-84 contains words related to religion and spirituality.

75

In this exercise, you will identify the ones that have meaning to you—either positive or negative. This will be raw material for exercises 2 and 3.

Open your journal to a new page. Begin scanning the list to get a feel for the content. Notice words that jump out at you. Then go over the list again. On one side of your journal page, write down ten or twelve words that *alienate* you from your spiritual life. Then go over the list again. On the other side of the page, write ten or twelve words that *connect* you to your spirit. Ignore words with no importance to you.

See if you want to make any changes. When you think you've identified words that have an impact on you, go over your lists again. Now put an asterisk (*) next to two or three words that are especially powerful for you.

EXERCISE 2:
EXPLORE RELATIONSHIPS BETWEEN THE WORDS

The purpose of this exercise is to help you explore relationships between language that alienates you from your spirit and language that connects you to your spirit.

Read the directions first. Gather the materials you will need: a large sheet of paper, some colored pencils and an eraser, and crayons or markers. If you want, use pastels or watercolors too.

With a pencil, draw a circle. You will be placing the negative words on one side of the circle and the positive words on the other side. Use color, placement, and size to express their meaning for you and their relationship to each other in whatever way fits. For example, if a word is very important, you could use large letters and a bold color to write it. If a word has both negative and positive meaning for you, you could write it close to the center. If one word overpowers others, you might write it over them. If some words are related, place them close together or link them. If some words conflict, write them far apart or use a symbol like a jagged line to express this. Take your time to design this diagram to fit your emerging awareness.

Now think about the two parts of the circle. Do the negatives or the positives take up more room? How sharp is the difference? Draw a line

76

or a series of lines to represent the relationship between the two halves. If you make a very sharp distinction between the two kinds of words, you may need a heavy line. If you feel more of a sense of openness, transition, or confusion, you might use a light dotted line.

Now, if you wish, use colors to complete the picture. You could shade parts of it with crayons, watercolors, or pastels to express yourself more fully.

When you've finished, look over your drawing. What feelings do you notice when you look at the circle as a whole? At each half? What did you learn from this exercise about the voice of your soul? ✍

EXERCISE 3:
I LOVE THIS WORD/I HATE THIS WORD

In this exercise you will be exploring in depth one spiritual or religious word that gives you strong positive feelings, and another that gives you strong negative feelings.

A Word I Love

Select a positive word from your list and write it at the top of a page in your journal. If you wish, use markers or crayons to decorate this word. Try saying it aloud a few times. How do you feel when you speak this word? When you hear it? Allow yourself to savor these sensations and emotions. ✍

Reflect for a few moments on the meaning and impact of this word on your spirit. When you're ready, write about the word. What is this word's gift to your spirit? What does it express to or about you? Does it remind you of someone or something? Write as much as you wish, using details to enliven your awareness. ✍

Try writing a few sentences that include this word. How do you experience your soul's voice when you write them? Try reading them aloud and notice what happens within. ✍

You may think of other experiments to try with this beloved word. Give yourself permission to carry them out and to notice their effects on your spirit. Let yourself engage with your word in whatever creative and playful ways occur to you.

When you're ready to stop exploring, take time to reflect on what this exercise has disclosed. Write about or draw your reactions to this entire experience. ✍

A Word I Hate

Select a strongly negative word from your list and write it at the top of a new page. Use markers or crayons to decorate it. Try saying it aloud a few times. How do you feel when you speak this word? When you hear it? Allow yourself the time to feel these sensations and emotions. ✍

Reflect on the meaning and impact of this word on the life of your spirit. When you are ready, write why you hate this word. Try to be spontaneous. Pay as little heed to your "no-talk" rule as you can, and tell the complete truth about your relationship with this word. What does it remind you of? Who does it bring to mind? What scenes do you picture? How has your soul been stifled by this word? ✍

As you explore your relationship with this word, you will probably find that it has several layers of meaning. In writing about each layer, you may find that you naturally come to a stop. If you do, pause to see if another layer appears. Continue in this way until you feel that you have said all you have to say about this word and its impact on your spiritual life. ✍

Reflect on whatever this exercise has disclosed. Write about or draw your reactions to the exercise as a whole. ✍

WORDS RELATED TO RELIGION OR SPIRITUALITY

A
abnegation
Abraham
absolution
abstinence
abundance
acolyte
Adonai
Advent
afikomen
agnostic
Agnus Dei
Aleinu
aliyah
Allah
All Saints' Day
All Souls' Day
altar
altar call
Amidah
anatta
angel(s)
anicca
Arhat
Armageddon
atheist
Atman
atonement
awe

B
baptism
bar mitzvah

bat mitzvah
Beelzebub
benediction
berachah
Bhagavad-Gita
Bible
Bible school
Bikkur cholim
bimah
birth
bishop
Blessed Virgin Mary
bliss
bodhi
Bodhisattva
body and blood
born-again
Brahman
bread and wine
Bris
Brith milah
brother
Buddha
Buddhist

C
candles
cantor
catechism
Catholic
CCD class
celebrate
celebration

celibacy
center
centered
centering
chalice
challah
Chametz
chant
chanting
charismatic
charity
Chassidim
chastity
chevra tefila
Christ
Christian
Christmas
chuppah
church
circle
circumcision
commandments
communion
community
confession
confirmation
congregation
contemplation
contrition
convert
conversion
covenant
creation

Creator
creed
cross
Crucifixion
cult
cycles

D
dance
Day of Reckoning
damnation
daven
Day of Atonement
deacon
Deeper Self
denomination
  (specify)

_____

_____

the Devil
Diaspora
the Divine
dharma
doctrine
dogma
dreidel
drum
dukkha

E
earth
Easter
Eightfold Path
El

Elohim
energy
enlightenment
Epiphany
Epistle
equinox
Eretz Yisrael
Eternal Light
ethics
Eucharist
evangelical
exile
Exodus
exorcism
extreme unction

F
faith
faith healing
fasting
Father
fear of the Lord
Feast of Weeks
five pillars
font
forgiveness
four directions
four elements
Four Noble Truths
four questions
fundamentalist
funeral

G
Gaia

Gemara
gifts
giveaway
Gloria
gmilut chassidim
God
G-D
Goddess
God/dess
God the Father
God's will
Golden Rule
Good Friday
Gospel
grace
gratitude
Great Mother
grounding
guardian angel
guidance
guru

H
Haggadah
Hail Mary
hajj
Halacha
hamentaschen
Hanukkah
harmony
Hasidic
Havdalah
healing
heaven

Hebrew (language)
Hebrew Bible
Hebrew calendar
Hebrews (people)
Hebrew school
hell
hierarchy
Higher Power
Higher Self
High Holy Days
Hijra
Holocaust
holy
holy day of
    obligation
Holy Ghost
Holy Spirit
holy water
Holy Week
homily
Host
hymn(s)
    (specify)

———————————

———————————

hypocrite

I
idolatry
Immanuel
incarnation
incense
indulgence

infallibility
inner awareness
inner reality
inner truth
inner voice
intuition
Isaac
Islam
Israel

J
Jacob
janna
Jehovah
Jerusalem
Jesus
Jesus Christ
Jew
Jewish
jihad
Joseph (St.)
journey
joy
Judgment Day
justice

K
Ka'ba
kabbala
Kaddish
Kali
karma
kashruth
kiddush
kiddushin

kingdom of
    God/Heaven
kipa
kiss of peace
kittel
koan
Kol Nidre
Koran
kosher
Krishna
Kyrie

L
last rites
Last Supper
Lent
liberation
litany
liturgy
Lord's Prayer

M
Magen David
Mahdi
mandala
mantra
maror
Mary
matzah
Mass
maya
mazel tov
meaning
Mecca
mechitzah

Medina
meditation
meditate
menorah
Messiah
mezuzah
midrash
mikvah
Minhah
minyan
minister
miracle
Mishnah
mitzvah
mitzvot
Mohammed
mohel
moksha
monk
monsignor
moon
mosque
Mother
mortal sin
Moses
Muslim
mystery
mystic(s)
 (specify)

—————————

—————————

mystical
myth

N
naming ceremony
nature
Ner Tamid
New Testament
99 names
nun

O
obedience
Old Testament
ordination
organ music
original sin
orthodox
Our Father

P
Palm Sunday
parish
Passover
pastor
path
peace
penance
Pentateuch
Pentecost
Pesach
pew
pilgrimage
pope
poverty
powwow
praise
prayer

priest
prophet(s)
 (specify)

—————————

—————————

prosperity
Protestant
Psalm(s)
 (specify)

—————————

—————————

pulpit
purgatory
Purim

Q
Qur'an
quest

R
rabbi
Ramadan
reconciliation
rector
redeemer
redemption
regeneration
reincarnation
rejoice
religion
repentance
Resurrection
retreat

revival
ritual
robes
Rosary
Rosh Hashanah
Rosh Hodesh
roshi

S

sabbath
sacraments
sacred
sacred space
sacristy
saint(s)
   (specify)

_____

_____

salvation
samadhi
samsara
sanctuary
sannyasi
Sangha
Satan
satori
savior
Seder
seeker
seminary
sermon
services
seven deadly sins

Shabbat
Shaddai
shahadah
shalom
Shavuoth
Shekinah
Sheol
Shiva
Shoah
shofar
shrine
shul
siddur
sign of the cross
Simchat Torah
sin(s)
sinful
sister
Skanda
solstice
Sophia
soul
speaking in tongues
spirit
spirit guides
spirituality
Stations of the Cross
sukkah
Sukkot
Sunday school
supplication
surrender
sutra

symbol
synagogue
synchronicity
synergy

T

tabernacle
t'ai chi ch'uan
Tajwid
Talmud
tallit
Tanakh
teffillin
temple
temptation
Ten
   Commandments
tikkun olam
tithe
Torah
totem
transcendental
   meditation
transformation
Trinity
truth
trust
tsimmes
tzaddik
tzitzit

U

unleavened bread
Upanishads

V	will of God	yoga
values	wisdom	Yom Kippur
Veda	wisdom figures	
vestments	witchcraft	*Z*
venial sin	witness	zaddik
Virgin Mary	works	zakat
Vishnu	worship	zazen
vision	wrath of God	Zion
vision quest		
vocation	*Y*	*Others*
vows	Yahweh	_____
	Yom HaShoah	_____
W	yom tov	_____
Wali	yarmulke	_____
washed in the	yeshiva	_____
blood	Yiddish	_____
Wailing Wall	Yigdal	_____
wicca	yin/yang	_____

REFLECTION AND INTEGRATION

Feel free to rest and let your experiences so far percolate. When you're ready to go ahead, recenter yourself using a Passageway exercise or any other method that works well for you.

Now look over the notes or drawings you've made. You will probably notice things that weren't obvious until now: patterns, repetitions, combinations of words or ideas, missing words. If you do, make a note of them. ✍

As you sit quietly with your work, you may have new insights. Write about or draw them in any way that fits for you. You may find it helpful to write your response to the following questions: ✍

- At present, who or what encourages you to speak with the voice of your spirit?

84

- Which experiences, ideas, or persons in your life silence or dampen the voice of your spirit?
- What remains taboo for your soul's voice, or what is still shrouded in silence?
- What needs to be healed to free your soul's voice to speak? What help would you need to heal this wound?
- Is there anyone with whom you would like to share some of what you have discovered in this chapter? Make a note of any person(s) who might be receptive and safe. If you wish, note also what you might want to share with each.
- Is there anything from this chapter that you would like to pursue further? Experiment with? Is there any theme or question that you would like to explore in depth over a given period?

Our soul's voice is our guide to a personally authentic spiritual language. As we begin to speak again about the life of our spirit, we will be able to enter wholeheartedly into dialogue with other seekers. We will be able to search out a spiritual community in which we feel at home. And we will discover new and vital forms of prayer that truly express our unique relationship with the sacred.

REFERENCES

1. Luke 19:28-40.
2. Prov. 13:24.
3. Col. 3:18.
4. Gen. 19, Lev. 18:23 and 20:13, Rom. 1:24-27, 1 Cor. 6:9-10, 1 Tim 1:8-11.

6.

IMAGES OF GOD AND THE SACRED:
WINDOWS INTO THE SACRED

*To say that God is Infinite is to say that [God] may be apprehended
and described in an infinity of ways. That Circle whose centre
is everywhere and whose circumference is nowhere, may be
approached from every angle with a certainty of being found.*
—*Evelyn Underhill*

Often, finding a spiritual path takes an erratic course. We start out with
enthusiasm on a new road: a new form of prayer, a new spirituality
group, a new religious community. We feel ourselves come to life. We
think that we have finally found a spiritual home. After some time, however, our enthusiasm may wane. We may feel stuck, disillusioned, or bored.
Discouraged, we may drift away, only to begin again some time later.

If we look a little deeper within when we begin to drift, we may find
that despite the techniques, practices, or community we've adopted, we
lack a true sense of an ongoing, meaningful, and steadfast relationship with
God, as we understand God. This is hard to admit to ourselves, much less
others. We wonder, Does everyone but me feel some connection with the
sacred? Am I longing for something that is unrealistic? We may feel lost,
confused, and often, ashamed. We may find that we can't put our finger
on what is missing, but we know we feel discouraged or even hopeless.

Our images of God live at the heart of our spiritual life. They powerfully influence our inner feeling of safety or danger as we recover and grow spiritually. They may silence the voice of our spirit, or give it freedom to speak. They may nurture our prayer, or impede it. They may open us to ritual or worship, or frighten us away.

You may find what I am about to suggest hard to swallow at first, but I hope you will hear me out. My own experiences and those of people I have worked with have taught me that the source of much of our spiritual struggle is childhood images of God, images that are often invisible, even to us. To survive pain from childhood and to sustain ourselves as adults, we have disowned images of the God we remember. We may have repressed them because the God we knew in childhood was terrifying. We may have discarded them, at least consciously, because they did not seem to square with our own experience. We may have cut ourselves off from them because they seemed childish to us. As a protest against the wounds inflicted by others and their religion, we may have rejected their God.

However, God, as we visualized or conceptualized God as children, is very much a part of our adult spiritual journey. Every image of God tells us a story about what will happen if we allow ourselves to enter wholeheartedly into a relationship with the divine. Every image evokes emotions; we may feel afraid, angry, touched, cared for, shameful, lonely, confused. Every image tells us the overall tone and qualities we can expect in our relationship with God. God may be close or far away, caring or detached, accepting or judging, just or capricious, forgiving or hard-hearted.

The images we've disowned block our path to an authentic relationship with the holy. When we reconnect with them—and with the child inside who originally had them—we find that they give way to fresh images which allow us to know and feel the sacred in new, life-giving ways. This is the first part of the healing process in relation to our images of God.

On our spiritual paths, we come to trust the principle that if we are to thrive, we must often retrace our steps and gain an understanding of what stunted our growth. The same principle guides me—and I hope it will guide you—in this chapter. My objective is to help you become more aware of the images of God that you carry within so that your relationship with the divine can flourish.

88

SOURCES OF EARLY IMAGES OF GOD

I was in third grade when I first heard Psalm 139. I was sitting with my parents in one of the front pews on the right side of the church. The line that struck me was, "In your book were written all the days that were formed for me, when none of them yet existed."[1] I immediately pictured a large library overflowing with books. In the library were an old man with a beard (God) and several angels complete with large white wings. The angels were taking books down and making entries in them, then replacing them on the shelves. I recall wondering how God could keep track of all those days and whether he (for it was a male image) ever made mistakes. This is the first image of God I remember. As I think about it now, I clearly see how much it was shaped by my experience up to that point.

My family belonged to a church where God was never presented in a scary way—hence, my freedom to be curious and to question. I heard Psalm 139 in church rather than in Sunday school because my parents allowed their children to choose which we would attend. The library I pictured was similar to my father's law library; the angels' record-keeping system was a version of the system the local bookmobile used to check out books. My image of God and the hardworking angels fit nicely with the energetic and work-oriented tone set by my family. My experience of my parents—in this case, my father, who was somewhat distant and objective at that time—also contributed to the image. To some extent, my personality and temperament shaped it. I was probably captured by the part of the psalm that involved books because I loved to read. And I recognize my adult self in this child who was thinking critically about whether God could make mistakes. Finally, my cultural inheritance provided pictures and other scripture passages in which God is depicted as an old man. (With only rare exceptions, most of us by age five picture God as an old man.[2])

OUR PARENTS (OR CAREGIVERS)

Our earliest images of God were drawn primarily from our experiences with our primary caregivers—usually our parent or parents.[3] If when we were infants and young children, our parents were gentle and responsive to our needs, our earliest image of God will be that of one who is loving and trustworthy. If our parents were physically or emotionally absent and uninvolved, the God of our childhood no doubt is disengaged as well.

OTHER ADULTS

As we grew, other adults cared for and related to us, so their qualities also molded our early image of God. We may have spent time with a loving grandparent or a warm aunt or uncle, for example. However, as adults, we have no idea that some of the qualities we now attribute to God are actually drawn from our childhood experiences with adults, because image creation is largely an unconscious process.

OUR FAMILY'S RELIGIOUS ORIENTATION

When we were old enough, our images of God began to be shaped by the religious tradition and affiliation of our family. A religious upbringing usually has at least three components. First, each religious tradition stresses some qualities of God over others. Second, each local church emphasizes some images over others. Third, each family either amplifies or tempers these images. The following is an account of how one woman's experience with her father, a minister in a fundamentalist church, combined with what she learned about God in church to create a frightening situation for her:

> The earliest picture of God I remember having was one of God watching me. There was always a sense that what I did wasn't good enough. I remember having a lot of fear about the idea that God sees everything you do. This was very mixed up with my father seeing everything that I did. My father seemed to know everything, to catch me at everything. I remember being very frightened by the thought that I just couldn't get away from being watched. I remember praying *God, could you just not watch for a few minutes?*

Children from nonreligious or antireligious families have images of God as well. Even in these families, children hear their parents discuss their beliefs, criticize the beliefs of others, or argue with other family members about God. Thus, children have to find their own way to reconcile conflicts between their individual experience of the sacred and their family's beliefs. In her memoir, *Finding God in the World*, Avery Brooke describes her solution to this dilemma:

> A ten-year-old has a passion for facts and for adventure, and these were supplied in abundance. But as I wandered over the hillside fields and through the woods, I sensed something more, a presence, a power for which I had no explanation. What was it in the sweep of the sky, the giant outcropping of rock, the sassafras leaf in my hand? I did not know, but I felt hushed by awe and a quiet joy. It did not occur to me to connect this "something" with God. My parents were atheists.... God, therefore, did not exist. I resorted instead to a two-layered handling of the subject. God did not exist, but I could allow myself to suspect the existence of an unexplained "something."...
>
> One day when I was visiting one of my new friends, her mother asked us to unpack a large crate. The crate contained her family possessions, well protected by layers of good old-fashioned wood excelsior.... I knew that the other meaning of excelsior was "ever upward." "That's it!" I cried to my friend (with whom I shared my atheistic convictions and my wonderings about the unexplained presence, the "Something" I sensed in the woods and fields). "We can call it X!"[4]

Even when a nuclear family is not religious, frequently the extended family is. Children may hear grandparents or aunts and uncles discussing religious beliefs and church events. They may attend worship services with them. Such experiences provide the raw materials from which children create and re-create their images of God.

THE CULTURE AT LARGE

In daycare and in school, children interact with adults and other children who have a religious affiliation and mention God in their conversations. In the local library, children see and read books that refer to God. In the culture at large, they encounter religious art, celebrations, music, scripture, buildings, and clergy. Robert Coles reports that even very young street children in Brazil have an active faith life:

> I worked with children in…Rio De Janeiro who were street children and therefore, unfortunately, by fate's decrees, don't have much of a home life and don't have much of a church life or a religious life in a formal sense. But some of these children were remarkably introspective and able on their own to speculate about God.
>
> Some would carry on extraordinary conversations with the statue of Jesus that stands on the mountain there overlooking the city—really poignant, at times heartbreaking conversations in which they asked him what he made of the inequities in the city, the injustices of their lives, the sad, hard travail that they were going through. Their minds were quite responsive not only to that statue but to their faith.[5]

How did your early experience shape your image(s) of God? ✎

THE THREE FATES OF CHILDHOOD IMAGES

Our early images of God may meet any of three fates as we mature. First, we may rework and transform them, replacing them with ever more complex and abstract images. Although we remember the earlier images, they have little emotional meaning for us as adults. This has been the case for me in regard to my Psalm 139 image. Over the years this psalm has remained an important part of my spiritual life, but my understanding of it has changed. Today when I read the verse about the book, I hear it as a powerful statement about God's commitment to be involved with me even before I was born and through every day of my life.

Second, we may have repressed our early images of God. As a result, they are not a part of our conscious awareness in adulthood. However, as we embark on our spiritual journey, they may come to light with tremendous energy. One such image surfaced for me several years ago during a meeting with a spiritual director. At that time, I had been experiencing a very powerful inner longing for God. I wanted to learn to pray, but no matter what I tried, I could not continue for more than a few minutes. I felt both frustrated and ashamed. Later, while writing in my journal, I described the image this way:

> I picture myself in my life here, and God is very, very far away—so far away that I can't even imagine the distance. It's like outer space. God isn't exactly human, but he's not an "it" either. He has human qualities. In relation to me he is benign—he is not dangerous or harmful. But he is not actively caring. No matter what I feel or ask, he will not come any closer. He won't completely go away, but nothing I can do can make him care. He will never be moved by anything I do or say.
>
> This God just makes me feel despairing. Why should I pray to him? Why turn to him? He won't give a damn. No wonder I can't pray! This really makes me mad.

Until then I had no idea that I harbored this image of God within. In spiritual direction, I traced the image back to my childhood experience of my father. Gradually, the two became more separate and distinct. Then new images of God—images in which God was caring, responsive, and accessible—began to emerge spontaneously.

Trauma in adulthood often elicits repressed images of God. At age thirty-three, Katie was raped and beaten in a parking ramp. In the aftermath, she was tortured by thoughts that the rape was God's punishment for something she had done wrong. She could not understand why she felt this way, yet she could not escape her guilt. She agonized, "I don't know where this is coming from. I don't *believe* this! I don't even know if I believe in God, let alone this kind of God. Where is this coming from?

93

Why won't it go away?"

After talking it over with her older sister, she remembered that they had attended a Bible camp near her grandparents' home the summer after she was in fourth grade. The emphasis there was on sin and salvation, divine reward and punishment. Katie remembered having been terrified that she would do the wrong thing inadvertently and God would damn her forever. She had repressed this image of a severe and punishing God until the rape.

Third, we may deliberately reject our early images of God in adolescence or adulthood. The images remain emotionally charged, but we deny their power. Diana was very involved in the Jewish religion as a child. She attended Hebrew school and prepared for her bat mitzvah. When she was fifteen years old, however, she had an experience that changed her faith life:

> In the summer I went to a Hebrew-speaking camp for eight weeks in a neighboring state. It was my first time away from my parents for any length of time. We were indoctrinated about the Holocaust that summer—with lots of detail and pictures, movies, the whole thing. I came home paranoid for years from that experience, because all we did was talk about the Holocaust and the similarities between American Jews and German Jews—six million there, six million here, involved in politics and community, etc., etc. By the time I got home, I was waiting for someone to knock at the door and drag me away to a concentration camp.
>
> I remember my counselors asking me if I believed in God and I said no. I said I can't have a God who allowed the Holocaust to happen. I just could not make any sense of that in any way, shape, or form. And no one was there to make any sense of it for me.
>
> Today [twenty-five years later] I cannot use the word "God"; it's almost offensive. I had to go outside my religion to find a spiritual path.

Rejected images are often frozen in time. Diana described the God she had rejected as an old man with a beard—an image she had had as a young child.

Have your images of God changed over the years? If so, how? ✍

EARLY IMAGES OF THE SACRED

Since most children under age twelve interpret the world literally, it is not surprising that in this culture, nearly all of us at one time pictured "God" as a male, humanlike figure. However, most of us had spiritual experiences in childhood that we did not link with this "God." These moments of special awe and wonder, of love and divine energy, created images of the sacred inside us, images we often did not connect to whatever we were learning about "God" at home or in our place of worship. Here are some examples.

Sherry Ruth Anderson and Patricia Hopkins, in their book *The Feminine Face of God*, relate the story of Cho/q/osh Auh-Ho-Ho, a member of the Churmash tribe, as she told it to them:

> You really want to know who raised me? It was a peppertree at the end of our block, that's who raised me. A peppertree with a short trunk that came up like this, she said, scooping her arms out from her midsection. It had a great nest inside that was like a womb. Its branches swept out in different directions, and they went all the way down like a weeping willow. You could sit in that womblike space and look out at the world without the world seeing you. And if nobody was watching, you could sleep in there. I felt safe and loved and protected in that tree.[6]

One woman tells of her relationship with a special place during her childhood:

> No matter how angry and violent my father would be, no matter how much he hurt us, the land was always there. I had

a special place across the field. A little stream ran through it and there was a dark, smooth boulder next to it. I would go there after he hit me and sit on that rock and I would cry and cry. Then, slowly, after a while, I would start to feel better. Comfort always came to me in that place if I stayed for a while. I always felt better. This was about the only thing I could depend on when I was a kid.

If we suffered violence, terror, or intrusion in childhood, our image of God is usually linked—consciously or unconsciously—with our experiences of being hurt. Our images of the sacred, however, are often manifestations of our experiences of being loved, rescued, comforted, or enlivened. For this reason, images of the sacred are more likely than images of God to be sustaining for some of us. Often, they are just outside our conscious awareness. You probably identified several of your images of the sacred when you explored your spiritual experiences in chapter 1.

Make a brief note about any childhood images of the sacred that have come to mind. ✍

MALE IMAGES OF GOD IN PATRIARCHAL RELIGIONS

Whether portrayed in scripture, literature, poetry, music, or art, in our culture and most others, God is nearly always depicted as male. This one-sided view damages and limits women's (and girls') relationship with the sacred. Whereas men and boys can see themselves as being like God, women see themselves as fundamentally different from God. Since patriarchy assumes maleness is superior to femaleness, women see themselves not only as different from God but also as inferior to men in relation to God.

This supposed inferiority is seemingly validated by Judeo-Christian scripture, preaching, theology, and education, all of which reinforce the assumption that only men can lead and connect the people of God to God. Jesus, of course, was a man, as were the great leaders and prophets of the Hebrew scriptures—Abraham, Isaac, Jacob, Moses, David, Isaiah, Jeremiah, Elijah. In the New Testament, the four Gospels and the Epistles were presumably written by men. Thus, women in the Judeo-Christian tradition literally receive the story of their faith tradition through the eyes of and in the words of men.

In our culture, women gain access to God only through men, with rare exceptions. For centuries, only men could serve as clergy. Male preachers present male perspectives to women, male ways of approaching theological and moral dilemmas, and male authority in matters of the soul. Having had nothing with which to compare men's ministry, women have not fully realized how much the gender of the clergy matters.

The Judeo-Christian tradition teaches us to see God as a father, a lord, a king, a ruler, a judge. Such images prevent women and men from experiencing God as a mother, a nurturer, a companion, a lover, a guide. They hinder women from seeing themselves as being like God, as well as from receiving God's affirmation of their lives and qualities.

Nelle Morton, in her book *The Journey Is Home*, describes her experience of an all-woman worship service in which God was referred to as She—an experience that she found profoundly healing:

> The words used [for the divine] in the service were exclusively female words…. Near the end…the leader said: "Now, SHE is a new creation." It was not something I heard with my ears, or something I reasoned, or something I was being told. Everything seemed to coalesce and I felt hit in the pit of my stomach…. It was as if intimate, infinite, and transcending power had enfolded me, as if great wings had spread themselves around the seated women and gathered us into a oneness…. I was not hearing a masculine word from a male priest, a male rabbi, or a male minister. I was sensing something direct and powerful—not filtered by the necessity to transfer or translate from male experience and mentality into a female experience and then apply to myself…. That is the first time I experienced a female deity.[7]

97

One path open to both women and men is to learn more about the female and feminine images of God that do exist in the Judeo-Christian tradition. For example, the following quote from the Bible speaks of a Higher Power who is female and very accessible:

> Wisdom is radiant and unfading, easily discerned by those who love her and found by those who seek her.
> Wisdom hastens to make herself known to those who desire her.
> The one who rises early to seek wisdom will have no difficulty, and will find wisdom sitting at the gates.
> To fix one's thought on wisdom is perfect understanding,
> And the one who is vigilant on account of wisdom will soon be free of care,
> Because wisdom goes about seeking those worthy of her, graciously appears to them in their paths, and meets them in every thought.[8]

Another avenue of exploration is that of the Goddess tradition. Here women can draw on archeological and historical information about matriarchal (or at least not patriarchal) cultures and their strong, nurturing, and earth-centered goddess figures. In addition, contemporary poets and artists have given us images of the divine that embody female power and care.[9]

Individually, we can use our frustration or anger to deepen our exploration. We can muster the courage to search out the sources of our early images of God, even though they no longer fit for us. We can question and reevaluate our assumptions about the gender of God. We can experiment with new images, letting our responses guide us to a more authentic spiritual life. We can allow ourselves to claim and value what we know about the sacred from our own experiences. As we do, we will discover more complex and creative new ways to be fully alive.

In community we can support one another as we grapple with male-only images of God and search for other images. We can create a climate of respect for one another's journey—no matter where we are in the process. We can also respect people who express their inner experience of God through male images.

IMAGES OF GOD AND THE SACRED

As you connect emotionally with your early images of God and the sacred, you may well have intense feelings. You may feel ashamed because you think an image is childish. You may be deeply touched as healing or loving memories surface. You may be full of rage about what others have done to you in the name of a particular image. All of these feelings, and any others you may have, are markers for you. They reveal your inner places with potential for growth and healing.

To grow spiritually, we need to set aside our usual defenses and to learn all we can about our feelings. If you are prone to using intellectual critique to short-circuit your feelings, you may find it helpful to explore their sources in your personal history instead. If you usually protect yourself from strong feelings by repressing them, you may benefit from staying with a feeling just a little longer than you normally would. If you usually guard yourself by minimizing the importance of your feelings, it may help to remind yourself of what you have learned from them so far. In this way, your feelings become teachers.

Because new images are conceived in our soul and take time to take shape and be born, we need to challenge ourselves to increase our tolerance for the ambiguous and the unfinished. In spiritual recovery, you can cultivate patience and practice waiting. You can learn to welcome even fragmentary images. Your spiritual life will deepen as you practice opening your heart to the sacred in and around you.

You may want to try some new forms of exploration as your awareness of your images of God and the sacred grows. You can use drawing, painting, mask-making, or sculpture to express old or emerging images. Any of the Passageway exercises could help you engage your intuition in your search. You may experiment with new forms of journal writing to get a more creative understanding of your images.

You might want to try interacting with traditional sacred images from the Bible or other religious traditions, or images created by artists and composers. Your reactions—positive or negative, angry or calm, sad or joyful—disclose important information about what opens your path to the sacred and what blocks it.

Try challenging yourself to open up in new ways to the love of others. This can renew your awareness of the sacred dimension of life. For example, a relationship with a sponsor in a Twelve Step group may teach you about steadfastness. The Fifth Step of the Twelve Step program, or admitting your wrongs, may help you understand forgiveness or unconditional love. A loving friend may teach you about warmth in a way your family didn't. Reaching out compassionately to others may put you touch with an inner generosity that you've never known. Your relationship with a therapist or spiritual director may teach you about the healing power of empathy. All these concrete, human connections with essential values are reflections of the divine. Through your relationships with others, you see new qualities of God.

Since these relationships are ongoing, your images of God or the Goddess and the sacred have the potential to expand and change continuously throughout life. There is no need to unearth the ultimate answers. You can trust your own pace as you explore your images.

Before you begin the Passageway exercise, look over the exercises in the next section. Choose the exercise you would like to do first.

PASSAGEWAY

Take a few minutes to relax and let go of the concerns of the day. When you are ready, begin.

> Focus gently on your breathing. 🍃 Place your attention on some part of your body 🍃 your abdomen, your chest, or your nose, 🍃 where you can watch the breath. 🍃 Watch it moving in 🍃 and out of your body 🍃 in 🍃 and out 🍃 in 🍃 and out. 🍃 Let the breath carry you deeper into a quiet place. 🍃 Don't force anything. 🍃 Just let the breath carry you 🍃 deeper 🍃 and deeper. 🍃 Just breathe in 🍃 and out 🍃 in 🍃 and out. 🍃 Let your breathing carry you deeper 🍃 into a

quiet place 🍃 without effort. 🍃

Now call up the image of a safe place. This may be a real or imaginary place. 🍃 Wherever it is, it is a place where you are in no danger. 🍃 Let yourself imagine the details of this place. 🍃 What do you see around you? 🍃 What do you hear? 🍃 Can you feel the sun, a breeze, a soft blanket? 🍃 What scents are present? 🍃 Is there anything in this place that you would like to taste? 🍃 Is there anything you would like to touch? 🍃 Use your imagination to experience this place with all your senses. 🍃

Notice how you feel in this place, 🍃 in this place where you are absolutely safe and secure, 🍃 where no harm can come to you. 🍃 Notice how you feel physically, 🍃 emotionally, 🍃 spiritually. 🍃 Just let yourself have the experience of being in a safe place 🍃 breathing in 🍃 and breathing out 🍃 breathing in 🍃 and breathing out. 🍃

This place is inside you, always available. 🍃 You can use your imagination to return to it whenever you need to 🍃 or whenever you want to. 🍃 It is a place where you can be completely yourself 🍃 because you are safe. 🍃 It is a place where you can know what is true inside you 🍃 because no harm can come to you here. 🍃

When you are ready, gradually and gently bring yourself back to the present time and place. 🍃 Take all the time you need to make the transition.

Take time to reorient yourself and stretch a bit. ✍

EXPLORATION AND DISCOVERY

The exercises in this section will help you see and describe some of your images of God and the sacred in detail. The first one is divided into three parts. Each part will help you focus on your present image of God or another sacred image. The two parts of the second exercise provide a way to increase your awareness of your childhood images. The third exercise will help you compare the qualities you attributed to God with those of people who influenced you.

Do the exercises in any order. You want to digest one before you move on to another. You may change the directions to fit the exercises more to your own language, needs, and experiences.

These exercises can be very powerful emotionally. You may experience new insights and be very enthusiastic, or you may feel overwhelmed. I encourage you to be aware of the inner impact of each activity as you do it. Treat yourself with kindness and respect, being aware of what you need and what will allow you to feel safe enough to continue your exploration. If you begin to feel overwhelmed or if you find yourself mentally absent, take a break to integrate what you have learned and return to the exercise later.

EXERCISE 1:

EXPLORING YOUR PRESENT IMAGES

You will want to tailor this exercise to your unique ways of understanding the divine. If you do not make a distinction between God and other sacred figures, do part 1 or part 3. If the Goddess is more important to you, do part 2. Each part triggers different insights.

Part 1. God

Open your journal to a new page. At the top of it, write "God—at present." Now look over the word list beginning on page 108. On one side of the page, list the words that describe qualities of God for you at present. On the other side, list words that definitely do not describe qualities of God for you. Feel free to add other qualities. If some of them seem especially important, mark them with an asterisk (*).

When you've finished, look over your lists and make changes you need to. This is the time for fine-tuning. When the two lists seem complete, look them over, noticing any patterns or relationships.

Now write about what you've learned and what you feel. Answering the following questions may help you focus your reflections: ✍

- What feelings do you have about God as you currently visualize God?
- Write a paragraph or two about how you describe God.
- What name could you give your image?
- Describe your relationship with God.
- Are there any conflicts or inconsistencies in your God?
- What surprised you about qualities you attribute to God?
- How old were you when you first learned God had these qualities? What was happening in your life at that time?

Part 2. The Goddess

Open your journal to a new page. At the top of it, write "The Goddess— at present." Look over the word list beginning on page 108. On one side of the page, list words that describe qualities of the Goddess for you at present. On the other side, list the words that definitely do not describe qualities of the Goddess for you. If you would like to add others, go ahead. If some qualities seem especially important or central to your current image, put an asterisk (*) by them.

When you've finished, look over the lists. Make any changes you need to fine-tune them. When the lists are complete, look them over again, noticing any patterns or relationships that are there.

Now write about what you've learned and what you feel. Answering the following questions may focus your reflections: ✍

- What feelings do you have about the Goddess as you now visualize her?
- How would you describe your image of the Goddess? Write a paragraph or two.
- What name could you give your image?
- How would you describe your relationship with the Goddess?
- What, if any, are the conflicts and inconsistencies in your image of the Goddess?

- What surprised you about the qualities you attribute to the Goddess?
- How old were you when you first learned or understood that the Goddess had these qualities? What was happening in your life at that time?

Part 3. The Sacred

Open your journal to a new page. At the top of it, write "The sacred— at present." Now look over the word list. On one side of your page, list the words that describe qualities of the sacred for you at present. On the other side, list the words that, at present, definitely do not describe qualities of the sacred for you. If you'd like to add other qualities, feel free to do so. If some of the descriptors seem especially central to your current image of the sacred, mark them with an asterisk (*).

When you've finished, take a few minutes to look over the two lists and make any changes you would like. This is the time for fine-tuning. When the two lists seem to be complete, look over the page again. Notice any patterns or relationships that may be present.

Now take some time to write about what you've learned and what you feel. Answering one or more of the following questions may help you focus your reflections: ✍

- What feelings do you have about the sacred as you now visualize it?
- How would you describe your image of the sacred? Write a paragraph or two.
- What name could you give your image?
- How would you describe your relationship with the sacred?
- What, if any, are the conflicts and inconsistencies in your image of the sacred?
- What surprised you about the qualities you attribute to the sacred?
- How old were you when you first learned or understood that the sacred had these qualities? What was happening in your life at that time?

EXERCISE 2:
EXPLORING YOUR CHILDHOOD IMAGES
OF GOD AND THE SACRED

Begin by taking a few minutes to place yourself in a relaxed state of mind. You may do this by listening to music or using a guided meditation, a Passageway exercise, or any other method that works for you.

Part 1. God

Open your journal to a new page. At the top of it, write "God—when I was a child." If you choose to explore your image of God at a certain age, note the age at the top of the page.

Now look over the word list beginning on page 108. On one side, list the words that describe your childhood image of God. On the other side, list the words that definitely do not describe your childhood image of God. If you'd like to add other qualities, feel free to do so. If some of the descriptors seem especially central to your image, mark them with an asterisk (*).

When you've finished, take a few minutes to look over the two lists. Make any changes you would like. This is a time for fine-tuning. When the two lists seem to be complete, look over the page again. Notice any patterns or relationships that may be present.

Now take some time to write about what you've learned and what you feel. Answering one or more of the following questions may help you focus your reflections: ✍

- What feelings do you have about God as you visualized God in the past?
- How would you describe your childhood image of God? Write a paragraph or two.
- What name could you give your image?
- How would you describe the relationship between yourself at present and the God of your childhood?
- What, if any, are the conflicts and inconsistencies in your childhood image of God?

105

- What surprised you about the qualities you attributed to God in your childhood?
- How old were you when you first learned or understood that God had these qualities? What was happening in your life at that time?

Part 2. The Sacred

Open your journal to a new page. At the top of it, write "The sacred—when I was a child." If you choose to explore your image of the sacred at a certain age, note the age at the top of the page.

Now look over the word list beginning on page 108. On one side, list the words that describe your childhood image of the sacred. On the other side, list the words that definitely do not describe your childhood image of the sacred. If you'd like to add other qualities, feel free to do so. If some of the descriptors seem especially central to your image, mark them with an asterisk (*).

When you've finished, take a few minutes to look over the two lists. Make any changes you'd like. This is a time for fine-tuning. When the two lists seem to be complete, look over the page again. Notice any patterns or relationships that may be present.

Now take sometime to write about what you've learned and what you feel. Answering one or more of the following questions may help you focus your reflections: ✍

- What feelings do you have about the sacred as you visualized it in the past?
- How would you describe your childhood image of the sacred? Write a paragraph or two.
- What name could you give your image?
- How would you describe the relationship between yourself and the sacred in your childhood?
- What, if any, are the conflicts and inconsistencies in your childhood image of the sacred?
- What surprised you about the qualities you attributed to the sacred in your childhood?

106

- How old were you when you first learned or understood that the sacred had these qualities? What was happening in your life at that time?

EXERCISE 3:
COMPARING YOUR EARLY IMAGES OF GOD AND
YOUR CHILDHOOD RELATIONSHIPS WITH ADULTS

This exercise, when combined with part 1 of exercise 2, allows you to compare your childhood relationship with your parents and other significant adults to your early images of God.

Open your journal to a new page. At the top of it, write the name of the person you wish to describe. Now look over the word list beginning on page 108. On one side, list the words that describe the qualities of this person. On the other side, list the words that definitely do *not* describe qualities of this person. If you would like to add other qualities, feel free to do so. If some of the descriptors seem especially central to your image, mark them with an asterisk (*).

When you have finished, take a few minutes to look over the two lists. Make any changes you'd like. When the two lists seem to be complete, look over the page again. Notice any patterns or relationships that may be present.

Now using the work you did in exercise 2, compare the qualities of God and the person you described in this exercise. Notice similarities and differences. Be aware of how you feel as you compare the two images.

Now take some time to write about what you have learned and what you feel. Answering one or more of the following questions may help you focus on your reflections: ✍

- What similarities do you notice between the two sets of lists? Differences?
- How do you feel as you review the exercise?
- What questions does the exercise raise for you?

If you wish, repeat the exercise for other significant adults in your childhood.

WORD LIST

A
abundant
abusive
accessible
active
affectionate
alive
aloof
amazing
angry
antagonistic
anxious
approachable
ardent
arrogant
astounding
attentive
authoritarian
available
awesome

B
bad
baffling
beautiful
benevolent
blank
bossy
bountiful
breathtaking
brutal
busy

C
calm
captivating
captivated
caring
cheerless
concerned
cold
comforting
compassionate
compelling
concealed
confusing
consoling
constant
content
cosmic
creative
critical
cruel
crushing

D
dead
delightful
detached
devoted
disappointing
disinterested
displeased
distant
disturbed
dogmatic

domineering
dull
dynamic

E
eager
ecstatic
elated
emotional
engaging
enraptured
enthusiastic
exquisite
extraordinary
exuberant

F
fake
fair
faithful
false
familiar
fantastic
fascinating
feeble
female
feminine
fertile
fickle
flawless
flexible
forgiving
friendly
frightening

fruitful
frustrating
fulfilling
funny

G
generous
gentle
glad
gloomy
glorious
good
graceful
gracious

H
happy
harmful
harsh
hateful
haughty
heartless
helpless
hidden
humiliating
hurtful

I
imaginative
impartial
impenetrable
imperturbable
inaccessible
incompetent
inconsequential

independent
inept
indifferent
ingenious
insignificant
inspiring
intelligent
intense
intrusive
invasive
inventive
involved
invulnerable
irrelevant
irresistible
irritable

J
joyful
judging
judgmental

K
kind
knowing

L
lively
loathsome
loving

M
malicious
majestic
male
masculine

maternal
mighty
mean
miraculous
mysterious

N
nearby
neglectful
nurturing

O
objective
obscure
offensive
oppressive
original
overflowing
overpowering

P
passionate
passive
paternal
pathetic
peaceful
persistent
playful
pleased
powerful
powerless
present
private
profound
protective
puzzling

Q
quarrelsome
quiet

R
reassuring
receptive
refreshing
relaxed
relentless
remarkable
remote
reserved
responsive
repulsive
rigid

S
secretive
securing
sensitive
serene
serious
severe
sincere
soothing
spirited
spiteful
splendid

steadfast
stifling
strong
stubborn
stupid
supportive
sustaining
sympathetic

T
tender
tense
terrifying
touchy
toxic
tough
treacherous
tricky
troubled
troublesome
trustworthy

U
unaffected
unapproachable
unattainable
unavailable
uncompromising
unconcerned

unfeeling
unmanageable
unobtainable
unreachable
unresponsive
unsatisfying
untouched
unyielding
upsetting

V
vicious
vigorous
vindictive
violent
vital
vulnerable

W
warm
weak
welcoming
whimsical
wise
wonderful
worried

Z
zealous
zestful

REFLECTION AND INTEGRATION

In the previous section, you focused on exploring in depth your childhood and present spiritual images and their relationships to the adults you knew as a child. Here you will reflect on what discoveries you made.

It may be helpful to take a break before you go further. A few hours or days away may yield surprising new insights. Or you may be bursting with insight right now! Trust yourself to know what pace works best.

When you are ready to continue, recenter yourself, using a Passageway or another method. When you're relaxed, look over your previous journal entries. You may notice things that were not readily apparent before: patterns, repetitions, dead ends, relationships, missing connections.

As you quietly contemplate your work, new insights may come to you. If they do, take the time to write about them or draw them. Allow yourself to work with fragments as well as clear insights. Some of these questions might help. If one question particularly piques your curiosity, begin with that. ✍

- What is the relationship between your childhood images of God and your present images of God or the Goddess and the sacred? Are they similar? Is one an outgrowth of the other? Are they incompatible? Do they seem completely unrelated?
- What do you notice about the similarities and/or differences between your childhood images of God and your childhood images of the sacred?
- How might your childhood images of God and the sacred enrich your spiritual life now? Is there anything vital or passionate about them that has been lost and could be reclaimed?
- Do your childhood images of God block or harm the life of your spirit today? How?
- As you explore the connection between your childhood images of God and your present relationships with others, what do you find is in need of further exploration and healing?
- How might you begin to seek this healing? Who might be able to help you with it?
- If you have a current image of God, the Goddess, or the sacred that feels right to you, how might you increase your awareness of it in your day-to-day life?
- Which persons and/or experiences in your daily life suggest new

images or qualities of the divine? Note them and the qualities of the sacred that they exemplify. How do you experience the divine through them?

- Which persons and/or communities in your life welcome and nurture your emerging images of the sacred?
- Did this chapter elicit anything that you'd like to do more thinking or writing about? Experiment with? Explore in depth over a given period of time?
- With whom (if anyone) would you like to share some of what you've learned by working with this chapter? What specifically would you like to share?

REFERENCES

1. Ps. 139:16.

2. James Fowler, *Stages of Faith: The Psychology of Human Development and the Quest for Meaning* (San Francisco: Harper & Row, 1981), 129.

3. For an extensive discussion of early childhood development of images of God, see Ana-Maria Rizzuto, *The Birth of the Living God* (Chicago: University of Chicago Press, 1979).

4. Avery Brooke, *Finding God in the World* (New York: Harper & Row, 1989), 1-4.

5. Robert Coles, interview on the *McNeil-Lehrer News Hour*, PBS, December 26, 1990.

6. Sherry Ruth Anderson and Patricia Hopkins, *The Feminine Face of God: The Unfolding of the Sacred in Women* (New York: Bantam Books, 1991), 35.

7. Nelle Morton, *The Journey Is Home* (Boston: Beacon Press, 1985), 156-57.

8. Wisd. of Sol. 6:12-16.

9. See, for example, Alla Renee Bozarth, Julia Barkley, and Terri Berthiaume Hawthorne, *Stars in Your Bones: Emerging Signposts on Our Spiritual Journeys* (St. Cloud, Minnesota: North Star Press of St. Cloud, 1990); and Hallie Iglehart Austen, *The Heart of the Goddess* (Berkeley, California: Wingbow Press, 1990).

7.

PRAYER:

COMING OUT OF SPIRITUAL ISOLATION

To pray is to take notice of the wonder, to regain a sense of the mystery that animates all beings, the divine margin in all attainments.
—*Rabbi Abraham Joshua Heschel,*
Quest for God

When I go trout fishing, I carry everything I need for the day in my multipocketed vest and fanny pack. I begin at a place where a river crosses a road and hike upstream on an angler's path, fishing as I go. Soon I am alone, with only the stream and the rest of nature as my companions. Fishing, I become one with my surroundings. I move carefully and quietly. At times, I pause to feast on wild raspberries or blueberries, enjoy the mating ritual of dragonflies, or drink in the fragrance of spruce trees and moss. Often, I just relax on a smooth rock in the sun, awash with the sights, scents, and sounds of the place. I feel in complete harmony with myself and all creation.

Occasionally, I encounter a dead end. For instance, a sheer cliff may block the trail, forcing me to cross the river in order to continue fishing. I know from experience that the fishing upstream will be better, because fewer anglers have traveled there. Often, I decide to make a crossing. I look for a place with shallower water and stable rocks. Sometimes I need a stout stick to help me assess the depth of the water and give me stability. Finally, I step into the water, picking my way from rock to rock as I cross.

For many of us, the spiritual journey resembles my fishing expeditions. We walk the path unhindered for a period of months or years. But at some point we reach an impasse: to grow in closeness to the divine, we know intuitively that we must begin to pray. Each of us comes to this crossing in our own time and in our own way, but for most of us, it is a crossing. We may have to feel our fear or anger in order to explore prayer. We may have to reevaluate outdated ideas about it. We may have to ask for help or expose our lack of experience.

Sometimes I decide not to make the crossing. If the water is too swift or too deep, or if I am tired or the hour is late, I remember the spot and return to it at another time when the currents are gentler or my energy higher. Similarly, you need not force yourself to explore prayer.

You can trust the process of spiritual unfolding to bring you to prayer when the time is right for you. At that time, you will feel a sense of attraction and ownership about your prayer life rather than a sense of obligation or oppression.

PRAYER:
A DEFINITION

What is prayer, and why does it seem difficult for us? We can think of prayer as *any practice that fosters or expresses our relationship with the sacred,* as we understand it. This can include meditation practices of all kinds. Early in my spiritual exploration, I refused to even say the word "prayer." Later, I wanted to use it, but the word would not come out of my mouth. I have since learned that many others have the same experiences and for many different reasons. So if the word "prayer" puts you off, consider substituting "meditation," "reflection," or "contemplation." You may want to replace the language you read here with yours. Find a way to stay with it even though your vocabulary may be different.

OBSTACLES TO PRAYER

When we pray, we actively seek a relationship with the divine instead of passively waiting for a spiritual experience. Being in any relationship means we have to make ourselves vulnerable or visible. The idea of praying can feel threatening to us emotionally, possibly even physically.

For people who have histories of abuse and neglect, closeness is often linked to being hurt. If we "see" God as menacing or indifferent, we probably assume that a relationship with God will end in our being wounded or abandoned. The prospect of being close to God or a divine presence, something exceedingly more powerful and uncontrollable than any human, fills many of us with *terror.*

We may refuse to pray out of *defiance.* If we were forced to pray when we were children, we may have shunned it to retain autonomy. If we were brought up in a rigid religious tradition—or in a family that stressed only the rigid aspects of religion—we may deeply resent the dictates imposed on us. If we associate prayer with harshness and severity, we may feel our spiritual survival depends on avoiding it.

It can be enraging to remember the hypocrisy of people who were supposedly persons of prayer, the same people who hurt us or did not protect us. Our *bitterness* might be preventing us from praying. A woman now active in Adult Children of Alcoholics shares this story:

> All through grade school my father molested me. He would come into my room at night. I would pretend to be asleep, hoping he would go away. At first, he just fondled me, but as I got older, the abuse got worse and worse. When I was a teenager, he was having intercourse with me.
>
> My grandmother lived in another town and we saw her two or three times a year. Three times I went to her and told her that Dad was touching me in bad ways at night. Each time she shook her head and said, "Take it to prayer, honey, just take it to prayer." At first, I did. I asked God to make my father stop molesting me. But he kept on, of course. I thought, "What good is prayer if God doesn't answer you?" I stopped praying for good when I was eleven.

The spiritual wound this woman suffered because of her grandmother's irresponsibility greatly compounded the emotional wound of her father's abuse. For many years, she directed her bitterness and rage at God more than at her father and grandmother for not answering her desperate pleas for help.

We may *despair* of any true benefit of prayer. Another daughter of an alcoholic father tells this story:

> I would pray that my mom and dad wouldn't fight. He would go and sit at the bar until it closed. Then he'd come home, and she'd come home dog-tired from working the evening shift and he'd be drunk, and then they'd fight.
>
> I can remember lying in my bed listening to them and praying to God to stop this fighting or praying that she would somehow get her act together and leave. Or that he would change or just have one sober day. Of course, it didn't stop until years later, when she divorced him. Somewhere along the line, I began to feel very punished. I got very angry with God.

In some families, prayer is thought of as foolish, and the person who prays is the object of contempt. *Self-preservation* might have kept us from prayer. Here's what happened to one man on a summer Sunday when he was about nine:

> We were sitting out on the front porch, which directly looked down on the sidewalk, watching families walk to church. There were two churches right across the street. As people walked by, Uncle Jack started calling out shaming comments, referring to them as the blind dummies, suckers for the Lutheran minister who was only after their money. The Lutherans, they were just basically stupid. But he would really tear into the Catholics. Catholics were crazy, believing in hocus-pocus. He would ask them how much holy water they

were going to have to throw over their shoulders today to get saved. He was practically rabid.

In this kind of climate, a person would understandably go underground with prayer or stop altogether.

Many of us link prayer with *weakness* or *dependency.* For men in particular, asking a Higher Power for help can feel like a failure of manhood. The same man, now a recovering alcoholic, had this experience when he was sober three months:

> I went to an AA roundup and a seventy-five-year-old man, thirty years sober, gave a talk. He made it clear that recovery is truly spiritual in nature and that without a spiritual awakening we don't recover. He made no bones about it and he talked about God. I was crying because I needed so much to hear this from a man and I had never heard it before. There were six thousand people at this hotel, but I found this guy and hugged him and thanked him.
>
> My wife and I went out to breakfast the next morning. I told her, "I want to be a man who has a God." I cried when I said it to her. It felt so good to say it, but I could feel this embarrassment at the same time. Part of me was afraid that she would laugh at me. I wondered if she would still want to be with me now that she knew this was what I wanted.

Like many others, this man felt he had to risk both his masculinity and his marriage to become more openly spiritual.

Maybe we are *ashamed* because we don't know how to pray. As children, we probably prayed for *things:* bikes, dolls, good grades, home runs, new friends. As adults, we are quick to disown this "childish" part of ourselves, knowing no one gets things just by praying for them, but we may lack more sophisticated concepts or practices. Despite the current trendiness of spirituality, it is still very hard for many of us to talk with anyone—sometimes even our closest friends—about what we actually do when we pray. Consequently, we may hesitate when we need to ask for guidance and information to nurture our prayer life.

ADULTHOOD TRAUMA

If we have been through some trauma as adults, we may have great difficulty praying. A rape or battering may cut us off from a well-established prayer life. Emotional pain—anger, shame, depression, despair—or physical injury may drain us of energy we need to stay connected to our deeper self and our Higher Power.

Sometimes our spontaneous prayer in the wake of a devastating experience is angry. We are angry about what we have suffered or lost, angry about being so powerless, and angry that God didn't protect us. Many of us learned early on that it isn't acceptable to be angry at God. If this is how we feel, we are probably cutting off the only voice that could speak freely and honestly to God.

On top of everything else, our family or religious community may insist that we pray for and forgive the person who did this to us. We are ashamed if we cannot bring ourselves to do this. We may accuse ourselves of having little faith or compassion.

For all these reasons, exploring and experimenting with prayer does not always come easily. When we reach the crossing place, some of us will step right in, while others will need to study the river for a long time. You can choose the method that works for you and take all the time you need to complete the crossing.

THE PRINCIPLES OF
RELATIONSHIP-BASED PRAYER

In the best and healthiest relationships, our behavior is congruent with our inner values. Our conduct is based on empathy, understanding, and respect. Our primary concern is the well-being of the relationship and those in it.

When we pray, we must allow ourselves to be true to our values and temperament, to the voice of our spirit; to be congruent with our image of the sacred. Our prayer reflects unique strengths, fears, gifts, and style that we would bring to any good relationship. It will be based on our inner experience rather than the rules and expectations of others.

As our personal spiritual language becomes clearer and our voice stronger, we can bring more of our real self to transform our old images of God; we can perceive our relationship with our Higher Power afresh and discover new ways to relate. As our life brings us new opportunities and new challenges, we can stretch our prayer to accommodate the resulting changes.

Affirming prayer as a relationship, we open to the depth and the complexity of life's most vital connection. We avoid comparing ourselves with others or evaluating our "performance." We recognize that our difficulties in prayer are not a sign of trouble but rather an inevitable part of truly being *in relationship*. We accept the certainty that in prayer we will experience dejection and bliss, closeness and absence, challenge and ease, agony and comfort. We come to understand prayer as a process that evolves as we live and learn, not an achievement or a technique.

MY PRAYER PRACTICES

Before I suggest a route to prayer based on these principles, I think it might be helpful for you to know a little about the ways I pray so that you are aware of the personal context for my thoughts.

Like many people, I need variety in my prayer life. Frequently I pray spontaneously in wonder at the bounty of nature or in gratitude for people's kindness. Sometimes I ask for an extra measure of courage or compassion.

Sometimes I use *vipassana* meditation techniques, in which you focus on breathing and observing thoughts, feelings, and sensations without becoming engaged or trying to change them. The Passageway exercise (p. 127) will help you with this prayer practice. In his book *A Gradual Awakening*, Stephen Levine explains these techniques more extensively.

Sometimes in prayer I express complaints, fears, frustrations, questions, musings, appreciations. At times, I ask for guidance or help. Often I include others in my prayer, calling them to mind and expressing my feelings about them or their situations. When I have a major decision to make or am struggling with a serious dilemma in a relationship, I often bring it into prayer several times for a period of weeks. I have learned to trust that if I continue to seek wisdom, it will come to me. If verbal prayer appeals to you, you might enjoy Ann and Barry Ulanov's book *Primary Speech*.

In the warm months of the year, I sit for about half an hour several days a week under a young ash tree on a bench I made with bricks and a board. In my meditation I open myself to my surroundings, to everything I see, hear, feel, smell, and touch there. Meditating in the same spot week after week, seeing the same sights as the seasons change, holds a special wonder for me.

Often, I pray using passages from the Bible, the *Tao Te Ching*, or scriptures of other traditions. Sometimes poems or passages from novels are catalysts for prayer. I reflect on how the story touches me and why, what it says to me at this point in my life, and what it invites me to spiritually. Macrina Wiederkehr, in her book *A Tree Full of Angels*, brings this prayer practice to life.

During the growing season, one of my prayer practices is "surveying the estate," a ritual I adopted from my family. Once or twice a day, I visit the garden, noting changes since the previous day. I soak up through all my senses the vigor and beauty of the buds, blooms, and fruits, and of the birds, butterflies, and bees that live among them.

When I journal as a way to pray, I reflect on how I have felt the sacred in my life over the past few days, or weeks. Often, I sit quietly for a while before I begin to write and return to silence occasionally. Over time, journaling helps me recognize the constancy of my relationship with the sacred.

I have experimented with many other techniques and methods. Some of them I found oppressive, or foreign, or abrasive—so I abandoned them. Yet I know other people who embrace those very approaches enthusiastically because they fit for them. My ways to pray have stayed with me because they are compatible with who I am. As you begin, remember that prayer expresses your unique relationship with the divine.

ONE ROUTE TO A PRAYER LIFE

It is important to provide yourself with the essentials for spiritual growth, or prayer can become an experience of self-abuse or self-neglect. You don't want to go overboard with spiritual practices that are harmful to you, such as extended prayer retreats or severe fasting. You want to be able to trust yourself to make sound choices, not rigidly follow a particular style of prayer that doesn't bring you any closer to your Higher Power.

Kindly self-discipline allows you to focus your efforts and energy so you can experience real deepening in your connection with a holy presence. You will need this so you'll actually set aside time for prayer and choose gentle spiritual practices, so you'll explore one practice in depth rather than many superficially.

To grow in prayer, you need to create a climate of *safety* too. Feeling terrified or guarded is incompatible with the sense of relationship that is at the heart of praying. However many attempts it requires, experiment until you find a way to pray that lets you relax and be open to the experience.

Exploring prayer requires *empathy* and *trust*. If one practice makes you feel bad, try something else. If you find that a prayer practice chips away at your self-esteem, give yourself permission to try something else. If you learned about prayer from a faultfinding writer or teacher, find a more nurturing mentor. If you feel ashamed or scold yourself, take the time you need—minutes, hours, days, months—to establish an atmosphere of self-care. Let this task be your prayer for a time. Make any change that will allow you to affirm and respect your efforts.

Finally, you need *dialogue* and *community* to sustain a life of prayer. You may seek out friends who encourage you and help you believe in your journey. You may find that a therapist or spiritual director can help you separate family issues from any impasse you reach when praying. And you may find it invaluable to talk with someone who already has a meaningful prayer life.

Developing a Prayer Life

Become Aware of Your Connection and Longing

The relational practice of prayer springs from the connection you already have with the sacred, from your longing to connect, and from your Higher Power's attempts to connect with you. To begin to pray, you need only to find the spark of relationship between yourself and the sacred and gently fan it until it begins to burn with a steady flame.

Begin by asking yourself, Where and when do I spontaneously feel touched by the divine? You already identified some of your spiritual experiences in an earlier chapter.

Often, the first movement we make toward praying is prompted by restlessness or longing. You may hunger for more time for stillness and contemplation. Something may seem to be missing in your spiritual life. You may yearn for a more personal connection with God. At first, it may be difficult to translate this longing into words. Treat yourself with kindness and patience as you struggle for a better understanding. Keep in mind that this longing is, in itself, a spiritual experience. It is destined to be, in some ways, beyond human expression.

Make a few brief notes about your connection with a spiritual presence—or your longing for it. ✍

Nurture the Connection

Once you are aware of your natural style of spiritual communication, you can begin to foster the relationship. Your relationship with your Higher Power is, in many ways, like your other relationships. When you are drawn to someone, you arrange to spend more time together. Prayer is a way to give yourself time with your Higher Power.

Several years ago, I criticized myself for not being able to follow through on a strong desire to pray. A spiritual director told me the challenge was not for me to be more disciplined, but rather to change my lifestyle so it was compatible with praying. Seeing the truth in this, I gradually carved out a forty-five-minute block of time three mornings a week when I wouldn't be interrupted. While your rhythm of prayer is probably different from mine, you too will benefit from setting aside the time to pray.

As you get more comfortable with praying, you will probably want to learn more about different styles of prayer, such as Zen meditation, centering prayer, transcendental meditation, or *lectio divina* (prayer based on scripture passages). Talking with others about how they pray may help too.

Sometimes prayer is as simple as bringing your full attention to a mundane activity. Being truly present to what you are doing often discloses its spiritual nature. Here is what happened when one man decided to focus on work in his garden:

> I was turning the compost pile—the leaves and grass and garbage from last season. You know, all the stuff we had thrown away. Over the winter and the early part of the spring it had all turned to dirt. Great stuff for the garden. I bent down and picked up a handful. I smelled it and it had the same scent that the air has right before a rain. It was so rich, so ready. Suddenly I found myself moved. To think that the stuff we had thrown away had become something that would make everything come alive! Standing there in the compost pile, I felt I was part of some ancient cycle that has been going on for millions of years.

Here are more examples of how people began to foster their spiritual connection that may help you select a style of praying:

> John remembered how close he felt to God when he sang in the church choir as a boy. He recalled how touched he was by some of the hymns. He set aside a short block of private time once or twice a week. He would spend a few minutes quieting himself, and then he would sing a favorite hymn as soulfully as he could. Afterward he wrote about the experience.

Joanie knew that flowers frequently touched her spirit. Each weekend she'd buy a big bouquet and take the time to arrange them, placing the flowers in several rooms of her home. As she did this, she would focus on the sensuous experience of handling, seeing, and smelling the flowers.

Reflecting on his spiritual experiences, Paul remembered when he was ten and his father took him to a remote lake in the Rocky Mountains. They hiked about eight miles and camped near a lake for two nights, fishing and hiking during the day. For Paul, this experience of harmony—himself, his father, and the surroundings—was sacred. As an experiment, he wrote the story of that trip in his journal. Later, he shared it with his wife.

Greg, a recovering alcoholic, felt himself drawn to the Eleventh Step of the Twelve Step programs, the one about improving conscious contact with God as we understand God. He went on a weekend retreat for men, where he journaled about the times he had felt in contact with his Higher Power and about people and activities that helped him to stay in contact now. He shared his new awareness with a spiritual director.

Whatever style of prayer you choose, check yourself to see whether the practice is helping you grow or is causing you to bring out survival strategies. If your prayers inspire growth, you will sense that you are receiving divine energy in return. Divine energy may come as new insight, or it may come in a dream. It may be a feeling of comfort or calm. It could be an experience of renewal or healing. Maybe it will be the gift of greater patience or compassion in a troubling situation.

You might need time to work on these first two steps toward praying, experimenting until you find a way that keeps you open to your true spiritual nature.

OVERCOME OBSTACLES

Nearly everyone encounters difficulties with prayer. Prayer leads us ever closer to the sacred. If we were abused, we may be terrified of intimacy with a Higher Power and wary of surrendering any control. We may be confused about what is normal in a relationship with the divine. Our religious background may have left us with images of God which imply that closeness to the divine will bring us only judgment or abandonment. Or it may have imposed on us oppressive and rigid rules about prayer.

While your journey toward a closer relationship with God shows your growing strength and health, it may be painful at times. Memories of traumatic events or emotions can occasionally intrude when you pray. If you get extremely restless or anxious during prayer, you may find yourself avoiding or neglecting a prayer practice you once enjoyed. You may find that you blame yourself when your practice falters, thinking you are stupid or incompetent. Even worse, you may see your difficulties in prayer as evidence that you are unworthy to be in a relationship with a Higher Power. These accusations are the remnants of past painful circumstances, not the truth about you.

Your task now is to learn more about why you have problems with praying. Perhaps the prayer practice you have chosen simply doesn't fit well for you. Many people struggled with meditation practices they thought would quiet them, but they only became more agitated and self-critical. When they found a more active style, their prayer came alive.

Your difficulties with prayer may have deep roots, however. By searching your feelings, memories, and thoughts during prayer, you might trace the connection to a traumatic experience. Most of what you need to know to resume your journey is probably just below your threshold of awareness. If you listen, you may hear the critical voices of clergy or parents. If you search, you may see old images of God. A woman raised in a fundamentalist church tells of her family-based struggles with prayer and meditation:

> As a young adult, I stopped attending church and had no spiritual life for about ten years, though I stayed in contact

with my parents. In my late twenties, when I moved in with my boyfriend, my parents quoted Christian scripture to the effect that I was a sinner and would go to hell.

I was hurt and angry, but I also felt relieved by their rejection. It freed me so I could reexamine spirituality on my own. I began to practice yoga meditation and write in a journal every day. I was very rigid about this. If I missed a day, I criticized myself and "made up" for it the next day. I constantly felt that I wasn't doing it quite right, that whatever I did was never enough. Though I was miserable during meditation, I was determined to try harder.

One day a friend who had known me since high school listened to my struggles with meditation. She pointed out that I sounded just like my parents: compulsive, rigid, harsh, never good enough. I burst into tears. In trying so hard to make a break from my parents' religious oppression, I had unknowingly continued to oppress myself. That was why I was so stuck.

Sometimes just becoming aware of how you have been blocked will clear the way to a renewed connection with the sacred. However, you may find that while you understand how you are trapped, you have no idea how to escape. Sometimes talking with a partner or a friend can reveal a way out. You might even need the help of a therapist or spiritual director to regain your freedom.

As you reflect on your experiences in prayer, remember that you are the ultimate authority on what's best for you. All your options are always open. Don't force yourself to continue with any prayer style. You can take a break for as long as you need to learn more or to reduce your anxiety. You don't even need to know the reasons for your pain or explain them to anyone before you make a change.

When you are ready to go ahead again with new insight about your own prayer, you will have completed one stage of your journey. Each new stage you go through will deepen your understanding, and your practice of prayer will grow in this spiral pattern.

Here you can explore your experiences with prayer and those who pray. Before you do the Passageway exercise, take a few minutes to look over the Exploration and Discovery section. You may decide to complete one or both of the exercises. For now, choose the one you would like to do first.

PASSAGEWAY

Settle into a position that allows you to be comfortable but alert. When you are ready…

Bring your awareness to your breathing. ❦ Notice whether it is deep or shallow ❦ fast or slow. ❦ Be aware of your breath as it moves in ❦ and out of your body. ❦ See if you can notice your breathing without trying to change it. ❦ Let your breath become the focus of your attention ❦ gentle and unforced. ❦ Notice how your breath feels going in ❦ and out ❦ in ❦ and out. ❦

When your attention wanders away from your breathing, be aware of where it has gone, without following it. ❦ Notice if you are planning ❦ remembering ❦ feeling ❦ hearing ❦ seeing. ❦ Simply notice where your energy is focused. ❦ Then gently bring it back to your breath ❦ without criticism. ❦ Just gently return to your breath ❦ breathing in ❦ and breathing out ❦ in ❦ and out. ❦

Let your breath be the place of return for you. If your mind wanders off, notice where it has gone and come back to your breath ❦ breathing in and breathing out ❦ in ❦ and out ❦ in ❦ and out. ❦

Notice more and more subtle sensations of breathing ❦ the air moving in ❦ and out ❦ through your nose ❦ your chest rising ❦ and falling ❦ your abdomen expanding ❦ and contracting. ❦ Be aware of your breath as it moves in and out. ❦ If you notice your mind has wandered, simply note where it has gone, without following it, and gently bring your attention back to the centering point of your breath ❧ back to the focus point. ❧ Breathe in ❧ and out ❧ with no demand for concentration ❧ no criticism for a shift in focus. ❧ Simply notice and return to your breath. ❧ Breathe in and out ❧ in ❧ and out. ❧ Breathe in ❧ and out ❧ in ❧ and out. ❧ Notice the details of your breathing ❧ and the movements of your attention. ❧ Notice without following. ❧ Simply observe the movements of your attention ❧ and return to the centering point of your breath without criticism. ❧ Just breathe in and breathe out ❧ noticing the flow of air in ❧ and out. ❧ Continue breathing in ❧ and out ❧ for a few more minutes ❧ in ❧ and out. ❧

Now gently come back to the place where you are sitting. ❧ Let yourself return to the room and to the objects in it. Be fully aware of your surroundings.

When you are ready, go on to the Exploration and Discovery section.

EXPLORATION AND DISCOVERY

Here you will explore your past and present relationship with prayer. Give yourself the freedom to write or draw anything that comes to you, without judging or censoring yourself. You need not be sensible, logical, or orderly. Let yourself be as spontaneous, creative, and messy as you like.

You may have intense emotions in response to the exercises. If you do, take time to identify and experience each feeling. Allow the emotion to give you important information about your relationship with the sacred.

EXERCISE 1:
EXPLORING YOUR ASSOCIATIONS
WITH THE WORD "PRAYER"

To do this exercise, you need a large piece of paper (11" x 17" or larger is best) and a pen. You may be more expressive if you use colored markers. For a better idea of the exercise, look at the example on page 130.

In the center of the paper, write PRAYER. Circle it. Now, as quickly as you can, write down any word you associate with prayer. Circle each word you write and connect it to the center circle with a line. You can include feelings, memories, names, ideas, or anything else that can be expressed in one or two words. Let the process flow freely. Do not stop to analyze. As you write a word, you will probably notice that related words come to you. Circle each and connect it to the word that triggered it. Keep going; put down whatever comes to you. Continue until you run out of words. ✍

Now look at your diagram. As you do, a few more words will probably occur to you. If so, add them to the diagram. ✍

Now take a break. You might want to stretch or make yourself a cup of tea. Give your mind a chance to rest. When you are ready, take another look at the diagram. Be aware of any connections or relationships that stand out. Notice anything that seems especially important or captivating. Take five or ten minutes (no more) to write about anything your diagram or the exercise has brought to your attention. Be spontaneous. Let the writing take any form that fits for you at the moment. ✍

When you have finished, again rest awhile. Then go over what you have written. How do you feel when you read it? If it makes you think of anything else, make a note of it. ✍

You might find these exercises helpful too:

1. Choose one word from your diagram. Make it the center of another diagram and explore it the same way you did with the word "prayer."
2. Write in more detail about any feeling or memory that has surfaced during this exercise.

EXERCISE 2:
YOUR HISTORY OF PRAYER
AND MEDITATION

This exercise is an inventory to help you identify the role of prayer and meditation in your life from your early childhood to the present. You may want to work on it over a period of time rather than trying to do it all in one sitting.

Begin with several pages, one for each phase of your life. For example, you may want to use five-year segments. Or you may divide your history into preschool, grade school, junior high, high school, and so on. Or you may organize it in some other way that is meaningful to you.

Begin with any phase of your life. Write down anything you remember about prayer or meditation during that period. How did you pray (if at all)? If you didn't pray, why not? How did you meditate (if at all)? If you didn't meditate, why not? What did you learn about prayer at this age? What did you believe about it? What were your struggles or questions about prayer? About meditation? With whom do you associate prayer or meditation at this age? How do the events of this period affect your prayer now?

Let these questions be guides for you. If other events or feelings are more important, write about them instead. Gradually record your history of prayer and meditation in each segment of your life. You may find that memories from one segment spark memories from another, and you may go back and forth between the pages. ✍

When you have filled in everything you can, set aside a block of time to read everything you have written. When you read it, write your feelings, insights, and questions in your journal. ✍

Here are some more ideas to try:

- Share your history—or certain parts of it—with a friend, partner, sponsor, therapist, or spiritual director.
- Identify gaps or questions you have about your childhood that

could relate to your background on prayer. Then gather more information by asking family members or others to help fill in the gaps.

REFLECTION AND INTEGRATION

You've explored your relationship with prayer and meditation in some depth. Here you can reflect on everything you have learned. Consider using the Passageway exercise to recenter yourself in preparation for this section.

Begin by taking a block of time to look over your journal entries and drawings. Look for patterns in your history, for threads of continuity. Look for abrupt breaks or shifts as well. Be alert to relationships between events and persons that may not have been obvious before. Check to see whether anything is missing.

As you go, make a few notes about your observations. Also note any questions that surface. ✍

Now sit quietly for a time. Notice any new thoughts, ideas, or questions you may have about prayer. Write about or draw them in any way that feels right to you. ✍

You may find it helpful to record your responses to the following questions:

- How would you describe your relationship with prayer now?
- Would you like to change your feelings about praying in any way? If so, how? Be specific.
- What stands in your way as you consider making changes in your prayer life? List ideas, feelings, experiences, persons, lifestyle choices.
- What kind of help or guidance do you need (if any) to "grow" your prayer life? What are some possible sources of help? Are you willing at this time to ask for it? If not, why not?
- Who would support you in becoming a person of prayer? Who might block your growth in that direction?

132

- Would you like to share some of what you have discovered with anyone? Name some people who would be receptive and respectful. You could also note what you would like to share with each of them.
- Is there anything you've learned that you would like to explore in more depth, either on your own or with someone else? Learn more about? Experiment with? Make a note of it, and make plans to act on it.

8.

FINDING A SPIRITUAL COMMUNITY: COMPANIONS FOR THE JOURNEY

When you see geese heading south for the winter flying in a
"V" formation, you might be interested in knowing...why
they fly that way. As each bird flaps its wings, it creates an
uplift for the bird immediately following it....
Whenever a goose falls out of formation, it suddenly feels the drag...of
trying to do it alone, and quickly gets back into formation to take
advantage of the lifting power of the bird immediately in front of it....
When the lead goose gets tired, it rotates back in the wing
and another goose flies at the point.... The geese honk from
behind to encourage those up front to keep up their speed.

*F*or whatever reason, many of us have learned to get by without rely-
ing on other people, by generally fending for ourselves. Thus, we do
not trust that others could nurture or support us. We don't know how to
ask for what we need from others. Spiritually, we grow as best we can on
our own. We may read books about spirituality, try out prayer practices,
or attend seminars or workshops.

We might avoid making any true connection with a spiritual community for many years. We probably don't feel comfortable attending
church or temple. If we are involved in support groups at all, we remain
on the fringes. Perhaps we've been invited to join friends in rituals or on
spiritual retreats but have turned them down. Maybe a traumatic experience made us believe that a solitary spiritual journey is the only safe one.

If we're people who have always covered up our feelings, we may be
understandably reluctant to join a spiritual community. Being in rela-

tionship with others in our spiritual lives means that we have to overcome the ways we have survived so far—concealing our real thoughts and feelings from ourselves and others, withholding ourselves from spiritual connection with God (or the divine as we understand it).

First, we must allow what we need and hunger for, and what we fear, to come to the surface. Although inner promptings can give us information to guide our search, they may also stir up pain and disappointment from the past—and often despair about the future. We may not know what we can expect from a spiritual community, or we may feel ashamed for not needing something from others.

At some point in our spiritual growth, though, most of us find that traveling alone feels restrictive rather than safe. It can be difficult to sustain prayer practices on our own. We may be surprised to find ourselves envious of friends who have found companionship in a spiritual community. Deep inside, we realize that our spirit needs constant nourishment and guidance.

This dawning awareness nudges us out of our isolation and toward self-knowledge and self-disclosure. Everyone feels the inner prompting in his or her own time and way. If we honor our feelings, longings, and questions, we will have a sense of clarity as we search for a spiritual community.

Searching for a Community

My search for a spiritual community may help you to follow your authentic path, whatever it may be. Notice and value your emotional and intellectual reactions—positive and negative—as you read on. They are windows into your inner world.

I was raised in a liberal Protestant church. An innately religious and spiritual child, I loved the music I heard during Sunday services. I was engaged by the stories and ideas I heard there. Ours was a warm community, one that welcomed children. Our minister emphasized the loving and compassionate side of Christianity. Our community valued diversity of belief and stressed respect for each individual's unique way of understanding God. As was the tradition in our church, worship was very simple and spare, focusing primarily on the verbal aspect of faith rather than on Communion. My experiences in this church gave me both the freedom to follow the promptings of my spirit and an interest in others' journeys.

As a teenager, I felt a gnawing hunger, a longing I could not even begin to articulate. My intense curiosity led me to visit a number of churches and synagogues and to read about many religious traditions. In retrospect, I understand that I was looking for a more sensuous, more ritual-centered, and probably more ancient form of worship—one that could touch me more symbolically and internally, more through feelings and senses than through the intellect.

When I was nineteen, I joined a different church. The liturgy (and, really, only that) had attracted me. I knew that I did not "believe in" many of the teachings of that church, but its Communion ritual moved me deeply. Through it I felt simultaneously connected with the earth, humanity, and God. I felt a spiritual kinship with the millions of others who have adhered to this tradition throughout the ages.

In my twenties, I began to believe that women were oppressed, both by our society and by the church. I began to think of myself as a feminist. My life in the church community was colliding with my relationships in the feminist community. Though my parish bent over backward to affirm women, the church as an institution seemed more and more inhospitable to my soul. Eventually, I came to believe that Christianity—not just my church—was inherently damaging to women. I rejected it and stopped attending altogether.

However, this was not to be the end of my story. I did not understand until much later, after I began attending Twelve Step meetings, that when I renounced my church, I had abandoned my soul too. In the Twelve Step program, I found fellow seekers with a set of spiritual principles who shared my struggles and accepted me without judgment. By example, the group showed me how to use these principles to reorient me to a spiritual life.

As I became more committed to prayer and meditation, I felt a deepening connection with an unnameable holy presence. In time, I felt the need to find a community of other seekers who could nurture my budding spiritual life.

I also participated in earth-centered and feminist rituals for earth holidays such as solstice. I felt a spiritual connection during those experiences, but I was frustrated by the infrequency of the ritual. At times, I even felt alienated.

I studied American Indian religions, and their beliefs and rituals touched a responsive chord deep within me. Though they are still a part of my spiritual life, I will always feel a barrier to full participation because I am not Indian.

In my early forties, I began to think about attending church again and to ask friends about their churches. Even so, when Sunday morning came, I couldn't get myself to church. One friend told me about his small and informal church, where Communion was every Sunday and sermons were delivered by members of the congregation, and invited me to come sometime.

I felt excited about the possibility of finding a community to support my spiritual life. But I was afraid too that I would somehow lose my way spiritually. These were my reactions, but I said only that I might come sometime.

Months later, my friend invited me to church again. I expressed my fears indirectly by saying that I didn't want to get dressed up, but he reminded me the service was informal. I said that I didn't want to get up early, but he said just to come sometime if I ever did.

I did wake up early one Sunday and went to the service, watching like a hawk for anything that excluded women. But I found nothing to quarrel with. The minister was a woman who used many images and pronouns to refer to God. The worship was similar to my childhood church but included weekly Communion too. I had found a church that had incorporated all the best for me personally. I had needed to know that persons with a wide variety of beliefs and relationships with Jesus were welcome. I found there the tolerance and welcome I needed.

I discovered that I had changed too, becoming more open-minded, less hasty to defend my beliefs. I was now secure enough spiritually that

I wasn't threatened by different beliefs. It took awhile, but eventually I went every week. I've been a member now for several years and know many wonderful people. I still take part in rituals of other communities too. I know that as I change and grow, my relationship with all my spiritual communities will continue to evolve.

You might want to think about your reactions to my story. ✍

HOW OUR PREVIOUS EXPERIENCES AFFECT OUR SEARCH FOR COMMUNITY

Many people begin to nurture a spiritual life only to have it wilt or fade out because they can't find a community that fits for them. Often people who feel wounded by earlier experiences start the search with powerful fears, doubts, and resentments.

FAMILY EXPERIENCES

Our family provides our first experience of community. If we learned there that belonging to a community means being terrified, we may have internalized the feeling that a community offers little of value. If we were mocked, humiliated, or sexually violated, we were trapped with nowhere to go. Joining a community may remind us of being trapped or losing ourselves.

Our background may keep us from distinguishing between harmful and healthy spiritual communities and leaders. We might not even recognize obvious problems or aberrant behavior, because it feels normal or familiar. For example, a survivor of sexual abuse may be vulnerable to sexual exploitation by a minister or someone else in a powerful position.

Sometimes a painful background sends us in the other direction: we seek the perfect spiritual community—one that consistently lives up to the ideal of love and solidarity. We may even think we have found it at times. When we see the inevitable imperfections, we may leave in disappointment or rage.

Sometimes we are particularly susceptible to a charismatic but tyrannical spiritual leader who demands unconditional allegiance. Or maybe family members cause us to feel so threatened that we can't develop a relationship with a spiritual group of people. If any of these sound familiar to you, write down how your family experiences have kept you from joining a spiritual community. We will discuss what you can do to change this later.

OUR EXPERIENCES WITH
CHILDHOOD RELIGIOUS COMMUNITIES

Childhood religious communities often teach us what we should expect from a community. Many people found their church or temple to be a sustaining force that softened the impact of bad childhood experiences or the pain of abuse and neglect.

A woman relates here how her church experiences gave her predictability and self-worth, which counteracted the chaos she lived with at home:

> The church I attended had lots of ritual, and the ritual was very meaningful to me. Things would be done the same way every time. I could count on it. There was a group of people who understood the mystery of ritual, how it used visible objects to point to invisible realities. That captured my imagination. During services, I always felt that I belonged there, in that place with those people.
>
> In the youth group, I was able to take part in services, speak, and lead prayer. I felt that I was just as good as anyone else when it came to communicating with God.

One man describes the sense of belonging he got from the church he attended as an adolescent:

> When I was about seventeen, I started going to the Disciples of Christ church in town. When I joined the church, there was a strong sense of family. That was important. I loved the sense of brotherhood that I found in the church. People

140

called each other Brother So-and-So and Sister So-and-So. I loved what that symbolized—the brotherhood of humanity. It was a tremendous sense of connection.

Sometimes a religious community aggravated the wounds we received at home. If this describes you, you might have a somewhat rockier path to community. Your church might have stressed judgment or punishment, creating a climate of terror. It may have given you rigid rules about personal conduct that were impossible to understand, let alone follow. If you were raised in a religious community that didn't address the needs and abilities of children, you probably concealed or denied your feelings in order to fit in. Perhaps persons of other faiths were seen as dangerous or sinful. The daughter of an evangelical minister tells what she learned as a child:

> The message was clear: Your close relationships should be with the saved rather than the unconverted. Because they are of the world and we are not of the world, we are the chosen, we are the special, the converted—we're God's chosen people. Some Catholic kids lived behind us, and they were the only kids we played with outside the church group. With them we had to be careful, because, the message was, our values were different from theirs and we might be led into sin.

Out of this experience, this woman came to expect a religious community to include some people and exclude others. Later, searching for a spiritual community, she placed a high value on inclusiveness.

Some people suffer from the conflicts with their parents' interfaith marriage. Sometimes there are abrupt shifts of religion because of divorce or remarriage. A woman describes how this felt:

> My first memories of religion are of first, second, and third grade at the Catholic school and the rituals of the Catholic church. They're positive memories. I remember my First Communion and feeling very special in my white dress. I just

felt kind of holy in the church. It was very positive for me. It was what I needed at that time.

This is what I lost when my mother divorced and remarried: not only my father and my family as I had known it, but the church as well. I still feel a lot of anger and grief about losing that sense of specialness.

Belonging to a church can make a family's problems publicly visible, sometimes leaving children deeply ashamed. Here's a story about a man from a small southern town. His father, a community leader, had had a long-standing affair with a woman, and the two had a daughter. They all went to the only Baptist church in town. He described a typical Sunday:

We would sit five pews up from the back, on the left side, every week. My half-sister and her mother and her grandmother sat toward the front on the right side.

My anxiety in church reached its peak when it was time for someone from each family to take an offering to the altar. Every Sunday I was expected to take it for my family. We all went down the center aisle to the altar and returned along the outer aisle, beginning at the front on the right side.

I always became aware of my father's tension when his daughter would come by. He had a very warm and loving relationship with her. She would look at him as she came by. Sometimes if he was sitting on the end, she would touch him on the arm. My mother would bristle. If I was sitting between them, I would feel the tension radiating out of both their bodies. This was a very strained time for me.

After the right side finished, I had to go around and deliver the offering. I could feel the eyes following me. The town was small, so everybody knew. It was like being in a spotlight. I wanted to disappear. I wanted to become invisible.

How does the church or temple of your childhood—or the lack of one—

affect your spiritual life now? Make a few brief notes if you wish. ✍

ADULT EXPERIENCES OF COMMUNITY

Because families don't always prepare children to thrive in the world, young adulthood was a perilous time for most people. Any unhealed wounds from childhood can affect every area of our lives—work, relationships, and the spiritual.

Many of us were lost souls as young adults. Without knowing it, we were extremely vulnerable. Looking for a safe place to belong and attracted by a predictable environment, we may have chosen spiritual communities that weren't good for us. For example, one woman, raised in a church she enjoyed, started to question it when she became an adolescent:

I had never been exposed to any other denomination. As a teenager, I started questioning. Why do I believe what I believe? How does what my church teaches compare with what other churches teach? I did ask my pastor and he just gave me a book to read. That didn't answer my questions; in fact, it stirred up a few more.

So when I went to college, I was looking for answers. I went to some Campus Crusade for Christ meetings. At first, I got answers. I think I was looking for someone else to give me direction. The people in the Crusade readily provided that. They gave me a clear list of what I could and couldn't do. For example, if you didn't have your quiet times and study the Bible for a half hour every day, something was really wrong with your spiritual life.

Initially, they were kind of nice. Later, they made me feel that no matter what I did, it was never enough. I lost my own sense of what was important to me because I was so indoctrinated with what was supposed to be important. It was very powerful.

For a lot of people, the spiritual journey brings us to the truth about ourselves—what we believe, who we are. For some of us, this means coming out as bisexuals, gay men, lesbians, or transgender persons. While some religious communities affirm those of all sexual orientations, others require secrecy as the price of belonging. One woman shares this story:

> In the early years of our marriage, my husband and I belonged to an evangelical church. Gradually, he realized he was gay. Suddenly, our circumstances weren't suitable to talk about at church. You just knew from sermons or how the members talked about these "other [gay] people" that all of a sudden you would be one of "them." Or you'd become a missions outreach project, where the whole congregation was trying to fix you.
>
> I really felt trapped. I knew my life needed to take another direction, but there would be heavy consequences. We lost everything when we left—all our friends, our livelihood, and our church. After we left, I had people come to me and say that I was on my way to hell because I wasn't going to church.

In exploring a specific spiritual community, we gradually become more aware of its beliefs, doctrines, and rules of conduct. We have more experience with its emotional climate, and our sense of safety may be altered for better or for worse. Conflict may arise between our values and those of the community at any point. A seminary student received a distraught call from a young relative:

> Visiting a church of her own denomination, this young woman became upset by an unfamiliar practice and phoned me frantically. "We filled out Communion cards to register that we were taking Communion," she said in a voice full of agitation, "and below the place where you write your name and address there was a little statement that said something like 'We at Emmanuel Church believe when you take

Communion you partake of the body and blood of our Lord, Jesus Christ. We also believe that the potential for harm in taking Communion is as great as its benefits, for if you take Communion without believing these things, you bring judgment upon yourself.'"

Fearfully, she asked me, "Am I a sinner because all this time when I took Communion I always believed it was a symbolic ritual? Have I really put my soul in danger?"

One woman, recovering from alcoholism, had faced the painful truth about the many ways she had hurt her children while she was drinking. When she joined a group that followed the sweat lodge practice of the Lakota tribe, her guilt made her feel unfit to participate:

I believed I shouldn't go into the sweat lodge with the others. I felt I wasn't worthy, that it was something I didn't have a right to participate in because of all the wrong things I had done in my life. Maybe I didn't want anyone to know about it. When you go into the sweat lodge, you bare your sins.

But somehow I knew that this group of people had to be part of my recovery. I had to find a way to tell them. Finally, I went back. I felt so vulnerable. I remember sobbing and sobbing. I was asking for forgiveness as a parent. People just listened. It was really healing. I had such tender feelings.

Have any of these experiences reminded you of your own? What shaped your feelings about spiritual communities? Make a brief note of them now. ✍

WHAT WE HAVE A RIGHT TO EXPECT
FROM A SPIRITUAL COMMUNITY

Despite these obstacles, as we follow a spiritual path, most of us find that we need companions. Yet past experiences might have left us unsure of what to expect and ask for from a spiritual group. Every spiritual community has imperfections. Yet for each of us, there is one that closely fits our needs and preferences and can foster our spiritual life. Not every community can accept every one of us, so it is up to us to search for or create one that can. Wherever we participate, we do have a right to feel safe. The doctrines of the spiritual community, its images of God or the sacred, and the style of relating in the community we choose should allow us to open spiritually. When we reveal information about ourselves it should be received with respect and care.

At the heart of any spiritual community are stories of humanity's relationship with the sacred. The scripture, tradition, preaching, and personal sharing of the community should resonate with our own story in a real, albeit imperfect, way. What we hear should move and touch us, allowing us to be more open with ourselves, other people, and our Higher Power.

Each of us has different spiritual needs. We may feel most connected to the sacred through conversation, scripture reading, ritual, music, silence, communal prayer, or other activities. The community we choose must offer much of what we need to thrive spiritually most of the time. This is not too much to expect.

Along with nurturing our spirit, we need challenge in order to grow spiritually. We need to learn more about ourselves, grow in our caring for ourselves and others, and examine our spiritual blocks. A spiritual community should help us with these, but not overwhelm us.

ONE WAY TO FIND A SPIRITUAL COMMUNITY

To begin, you must accept a paradox. On one hand, you will need to sharpen your awareness through reflection, gather information, and make responsible decisions. On the other, you will need to be ready for new and unexpected experiences, not try too hard, and be ready for the right spiritual community when it comes into your life. Though you might have to do some work to find a spiritual home, it's not really going to be an achievement, but a sacred gift. Each step offers reliable guidance only when you stay open to the unexpected touch of the divine.

REFLECTION AND PRAYER

Reflection and prayer can help you stay centered and calm as you learn more about spiritual communities. Your spiritual voice can tell you who you are as you start to look. In reflection, ask yourself: What do I need? What do I want? What is absolutely critical for me right now? What are my strengths? What do I have to offer? What do I need to guard against? Through reflection, you learn what has worked before. You can pray for guidance or enter a place of stillness within to listen for direction.

Keeping in mind the qualities that are most important to you, you may rule out some denominations, congregation sizes, or styles of worship. If you already belong to a church or other group, you can evaluate what is working.

As you reflect and pray, you can use writing or dialogue to honor your emerging wisdom and to remember what you learned. You can journal to follow your exploration and record the results. You can talk with someone and let this person reflect your ideas back so they are newly illuminated. You may be hesitant to speak your truth because it is fragmented, confused, or vague. But if you dare to give voice to it, you might find it offers fresh insights and opens the way to further exploration.

GATHERING INFORMATION

When you feel you know enough about yourself, you can gather information about different communities. One of the best ways to do this is to conduct interviews as you would if you were looking for a job. You can create questions and use them as a guide when you interview people. You may choose people in a support group, especially those you've learned from. Friends or acquaintances can tell you about their churches, synagogues, or spirituality groups. You can follow up with reading.

Unexpected opportunities may turn up for taking part in someone else's community. You might be invited to a Shabbat meal, a solstice ritual, a wedding, or a retreat. Watch yourself as you make the decision to accept or decline. If you take part, all your feelings and thoughts will give you information about your needs for community.

On your own, you might attend services at a church or synagogue, participate in a retreat, or sign up for a yoga or t'ai chi class. Maybe you could gather a few friends for an informal spirituality group. Or you might try a few meetings of a Twelve Step group.

Through the whole information-gathering process, you can reflect and pray to gain deeper understanding of what you're learning and what it all means. If you don't like some experience, reflecting on it will sharpen your perceptions about what didn't match your needs. If you are attracted to a community, prayer may help you articulate why. You may find rich insights in unexpected reactions.

You may need months or even years to gather information. You will have your own methods and your own timetable; you can work steadily or in spurts. There's no need to reach any quick conclusion. Everything you learn has value in guiding your future steps.

BECOMING INVOLVED

Your search will probably lead you to a community that will attract you. As you begin a relationship with this community, you can draw on reflection, prayer, and the information-gathering skills you have now.

Participating in a spiritual or religious community is an active process that requires many decisions, big and small. You'll need to decide what information to share about yourself and with whom. You eventually will decide when to join (if at all) and how you want to act on your commitment. Since you and your chosen community will always be changing and growing, you may even need at some point to decide if you will leave. Seeking spiritual community is a lifelong process.

The Exploration and Discovery section contains three exercises, each with a different focus. Take a few minutes now to look them over and decide which one you would like to do first. When you are ready, do the Passageway exercise.

PASSAGEWAY

Take a few minutes to settle yourself. Let your body relax. When you are ready...

Imagine yourself as a plant growing in a garden. Take your time, and let the image come into your awareness on its own ❧ taking shape gradually ❧ or all at once. ❧ There is no need to force it. Just allow the image to be born. ❧

As the image becomes clearer, feel your size. ❧ Are you tall or short, sturdy or delicate? Become aware of your form. ❧ Are you wispy or bushy? ❧ Be aware of your leaves ❧ their size ❧ and shape ❧ and color. ❧

Now turn your attention to your surroundings. ❧ Where are you growing? ❧ Are you in the shade ❧ or in the sun? ❧ In a large garden ❧ or a small one? ❧ Are there other plants near you? ❧ Touching you? ❧ What are they like? ❧

What time of year is it? ❧ Are you feeling the new growth of spring ❧ or the blooming time of summer ❧ or the seedtime of fall ❧ or the resting time of winter? ❧ Feel the light on your leaves and stems. ❧ Is it strong or weak? ❧ Bright or filtered? ❧ Feel the air moving around you. Is it chilly or mild? ❧ Dry or moist? ❧ Is there a breeze or a wind? ❧ Let yourself feel the air and the light around you. ❧ Now feel the soil around your roots. ❧ Is it moist or dry? ❧ Cool or warm? ❧

Let yourself experience the other creatures in the garden where you stand. ❧ Perhaps there are children playing nearby ❧ or birds singing ❧ or frogs croaking ❧ or butterflies flitting from blossom to blossom. ❧ Perhaps the gardener is tending the garden ❧ or picking flowers ❧ or harvesting vegetables. ❧ Maybe a rabbit or a mouse is nearby. ❧

Take a few minutes to rest in your awareness of yourself and your surroundings. ❧ Let the scene unfold or change ❧ or just stay the same. ❧ Allow yourself to relax in this time and place. ❧ Just rest in this spot. ❧ Now gently return to the present moment.

EXPLORATION AND DISCOVERY

In this section you will explore in more detail your experiences with community, both religious and spiritual. Remember that you are the authority. You know when and where you have experienced community.

EXERCISE 1:
EXPLORING YOUR HISTORY WITH COMMUNITY

In your journal or on a large sheet of paper, make a list of all the religious and spiritual communities you've participated in, leaving a space after each entry. Begin with your childhood church or synagogue and work up to the present. Feel free to include even brief contacts and any communities, such as Scouts or a musical group, that fed you spiritually, whether it was explicitly religious or not.

When you've finished, take a few minutes to look it over. Mark with an asterisk (*) communities of particular importance to you—either positive or negative—in your search for a spiritual path.

Now choose one of your marked entries. Take a few minutes to remember your experiences in this community, and then write your responses to some or all of the following questions. You can work quickly or slowly, but try to be as honest as you can. Include fragments that seem important, even if you don't know exactly why.

- How was this community important to you?
- What did you learn there about what it means to belong to a religious community? Include both spoken and unspoken messages. You may want to complete this sentence in a number of ways: From this congregation or group, I learned…
- How, if at all, has your participation in this community sustained you on your spiritual path?
- How, if at all, are your present spiritual struggles related to your participation in this community?
- What, if anything, did you learn or receive there that is still valuable to you? Be as specific as you can.

Answer these questions for one or two more of your marked entries. ✍

When you've finished, you may want to take a break. When you come back, look over what you've written. Note in your journal what stands out for you. If there's anything you want to add or write more about, go ahead. ✍

EXERCISE 2:
IDENTIFYING THE MEMBERS OF YOUR PRESENT
SPIRITUAL COMMUNITY

Turn to a blank page in your journal. Take a few minutes to quiet yourself.

When you are ready, ask yourself the following question: Where do I feel a sense of spiritual community now? (Remember that a spiritual community can include both people who have died and those who are living, people you've met and those you don't know.) Quickly and briefly write down everything that comes to mind. Let it flow and try not to censor yourself. Do not stop to explore or censor right now. When you reach a natural pause, ask yourself the question again and write anything else that comes up. Repeat this process until your list seems complete. ✍

Now take a short break to stretch or relax. When you return, add to your list anything that may have occurred to you during the break. ✍

Now go back over your list. Beside each entry, describe how the person or thing increases or strengthens your relationship with your Higher Power. Take all the time you need. ✍

Take another short break. When you come back, look over everything you've written. Be aware of your feelings as you do.

EXERCISE 3:
IDENTIFYING QUALITIES THAT YOU DESIRE
IN A SPIRITUAL COMMUNITY

Take a few minutes to focus your attention by using the Passageway exercise or any other method that works for you. When you're ready, reflect on the qualities you're looking for in a spiritual community. In your journal,

151

quickly jot down the qualities that occur to you. For now, try not to think too much about them; just let them flow onto the page. ✍

When you reach a natural stopping point, sit quietly for a few minutes. Note any other characteristics that come to mind.

Now, if you wish, use the list on pages 153-154 to expand your own list. Copy words that fit for you into your journal. ✍

When you feel that your list is complete, look it over for a few minutes. Which qualities are absolutely crucial to your spiritual growth and well-being? Mark them with a symbol of your choice. Which are desirable but not crucial? Mark them with another symbol. Now review your list again and fine-tune it. ✍

Take a brief break at this point to take a walk or drink a cup of tea or coffee. Stretch your body and allow your mind to wander. When you feel refreshed, look over your list. Write your answers to some or all of the following questions: ✍

- How do you feel about the work you have done on this exercise so far?
- What do the qualities you have identified have in common? How are they related? Is there a central value or idea that connects them?
- What are the conflicts or contradictions, if any, among the qualities you have listed?
- If you have participated in spiritual or religious communities in the past, which of your listed qualities, if any, did they have? Which did they lack? What were the dominant qualities of these communities?
- If you participate in one or more spiritual communities now, which qualities do they have? Which do they lack? What are the dominant qualities of these communities?
- What questions, if any, does this exercise raise for you?

Now is a good time to let what you've learned "cook" for a while.

DESIRABLE QUALITIES
OF SPIRITUAL COMMUNITIES

A
accepting
accessible
active
alive
approachable
attentive
available

B
beneficent
bold
bountiful
busy

C
calm
captivating
caring
challenging
clergy-led
close
concerned
comforting
compassionate
complex
constant
content
courteous
creative
courageous

D
dependable
dispassionate
dynamic

E
ecstatic
educational
egalitarian
emotional
energetic
engaging
enthusiastic
expressive

F
fair
faithful
familiar
feminine
feminist
flexible
forgiving
forthright
fresh
friendly
fulfilling
fun

G
generous
gentle
glad
gracious

H
happy
hardworking
hierarchical
honest

I
imaginative
impartial
inclusive
independent
innovative
inspiring
intellectual
intelligent
intense
intimate
inventive
involved

J
joyful
justice-oriented

K
kind
knowing

L
large
lively
loving

M
masculine
maternal
mellow
musical

N
nearby
new
nontraditional
nurturing

O
objective
old
open
open to conflict
original

P
passionate
participatory
paternal
peaceful
persistent

playful
powerful
principled
private
protective

Q
questioning
quiet

R
rational
reassuring
receptive
refreshing
relaxed
reserved
respectful
responsive
restrained
risk-taking

S
safe
sensitive
serene
serious
service-oriented
sincere

small
simple
solid
soothing
spirited
stable
steadfast
strong
structured
supportive
sustaining
sympathetic

T
tactful
temperate
tolerant
traditional
trustworthy

V
vigorous
vital
vulnerable

W
warm
welcoming
wise

REFLECTION AND INTEGRATION

Begin by reading everything you have written in the exercises. Note any new insights or questions that spontaneously occur to you. Then write your responses to some or all of these questions:

- What patterns do you see in your history with community?
- How are your present and past experiences of community related? Are they harmonious? How? Do they clash? How?
- Have there been shifts or breaks in your choices about community? How would you describe them?
- What's missing for you now in terms of spiritual community?
- What might be your next step(s) in exploring spiritual community?
- Is there anything else you have learned about yourself and community?

9.

RITUAL:

ENACTING OUR CONNECTIONS

Ritual is food to the spiritually hungry. Ritual has the potential to heal and warm; to glorify God and reify human devotion; to make objects and places sacred; to create community; to permeate the membrane between religion and peoplehood and bond one person into the whole. Ritual physicalizes the spiritual and spiritualizes the physical.
—*Letty Cottin Pogrebin,* Deborah, Golda and Me

*I*magine the life of your spirit as a triangle. The lower left corner represents your *personal history,* from your birth to the present moment. The lower right corner represents all your *personal relationships*—your family, lovers, friendships, work, school, and religious or spiritual communities. At the top of the triangle is your *Higher Power or God,* as you have understood it before or understand it now. In the center of the triangle we can represent *ritual.*

When we participate in a ritual, we bring with us all of our personal history. It tells us what we can expect and guides our mind, heart, and senses as we take in the ritual event. Since spiritual rituals involve other people, our relationships—past and present—color our perceptions and influence how trusting we can allow ourselves to be. And since many rituals take place in religious and spiritual settings, they awaken and may even alter our understandings of the sacred.

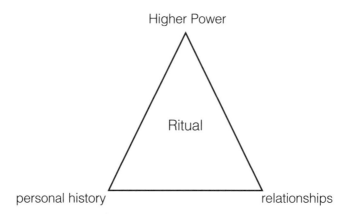

Higher Power

Ritual

personal history | relationships

Ritual will evoke our hopes and hungers in any of these areas. And because it frequently takes place at important turning points in our lives—birth, marriage, times of trouble, death—ritual has the power to reawaken the ache or the joy of similar events in the past. For most people, rituals can be intense experiences.

THE CHARACTERISTICS OF RITUAL

The many-faceted nature of ritual makes us vulnerable, because rituals touch us through our *senses*. Their impact often goes right past our defense system. The smell of candle wax or incense can instantly transport us mentally to another time and place. The sound of a hymn can bring out long-forgotten memories and emotions. A friend tells how he was unexpectedly moved at a funeral:

> I never went to church after I was about thirteen years old. In my thirties, I went to a funeral. I didn't know the man who had died that well, but he worked at my firm, so I was pretty much expected to go. The service was at the cathedral. Hundreds of people were there. The music was beautiful. I felt pretty tuned out until the organ started playing "God Be with You 'Til We Meet Again"—a hymn I had loved as a child. Before I even knew what was happening, I started crying. I couldn't believe it! I felt so many emotions; I couldn't even

begin to know what they were. It was like a reunion with some part of myself that I had lost for thirty years—very sad and very joyful at the same time.

Rituals make use of *repetition* to connect us with our spirituality. The order, movements, garments, words, and music are the same time after time. As a result, a ritual can become deeply ingrained and we resonate with it, even when we do not consciously participate in it. By relieving us of the need to attend to details, the repetition of a ritual opens our spirit to the many symbolic levels of meaning that all true rituals contain.

Rituals make use of *symbols* to express the realities of our relationships with ourselves, others, and the sacred. Some symbols are universal: fire, water, and food, to name only a few. Others are unique to a specific ritual. Whether universal or unique, symbols touch each of us differently, depending on our history and their meaning within a given community. For example, the wine used in a Communion ritual may give one person a feeling of connection with Jesus but threaten another person's confidence in staying sober.

WHY RITUAL IS IMPORTANT

In a way that nothing else can, rituals place our lives in a sacred context. Through our rituals, we discover and rediscover sustaining images for the life of our spirit, and we affirm the core values of our spiritual life. Ritual can be a powerful antidote to the distortions produced by painful experiences in the past. Rituals reaffirm and nourish our connection with ourselves, with others traveling a spiritual path, and with the divine. It alerts us to the sacred energy that guides and nurtures our spiritual lives, mending broken relationships. Writer Linda Hogan describes a traditional sweat lodge ceremony in which her perceptions of her place in the universe were fundamentally transformed:

> By late afternoon we are ready, one at a time, to enter the enclosure. The hot lava stones are placed inside.... After the flap, which serves as a door, is closed, water is poured over the

stones and the hot steam rises around us. In a sweat lodge ceremony, the entire world is brought inside the enclosure.... It is all called in. The animals come from the warm and sunny distances. Water from dark lakes is there. Wind...arrives from the four directions.... The sky is there, with all the stars.... It is a place grown intense and holy.... We sit together in our loneliness and speak, one at a time, our deepest language of need, hope, loss, and survival. We remember that all things are connected.... We speak. We sing. We swallow water and breathe smoke. By the end of the ceremony, it is as if skin contains land and birds. The places within us have become filled.... Inside the enclosure of the lodge, the animals and ancestors move into the human body, into skin and blood. The land merges with us. The stones come to dwell inside the person.... We who easily grow apart from the world are returned to the great store of life all around us and there is the deepest sense of being at home here in this intimate kinship.... We are a part of something larger.[1]

Rituals can offer comfort and continuity in times of trouble. Rituals break through our isolation, providing companions and a framework of meaning for life events that could be overwhelming. When someone dies, a funeral can allow us to celebrate life. When catastrophe strikes, sweat-lodge or Communion rituals bind us to something that has not been destroyed. Elie Wiesel, in his book *One Generation After,* recounts the sustaining power of ritual in a terrible and unspeakable catastrophe, being imprisoned in a concentration camp:

> We had decided to organize a [Rosh Hashanah] service.... We were determined to welcome the New Year as before, forming a congregation by the sheer force and concentration of our fervor. And the barbed wires? We would have to ignore them. And the jailers? We would have to defy them.....
> A cantor was found who remembered the Rosh Hashanah

service by heart. He recited it aloud and the congregation repeated it verse for verse. We felt like weeping…but we controlled ourselves until one of the men…burst into sobs. A moment later everybody was weeping with him.… We mourned the dead and the living, the vanished homes and desecrated sanctuaries, we wept without shame or hope.…

Suddenly an inmate stepped forward and began to speak: "Brothers, listen to me. Tonight is Rosh Hashanah, the threshold of a new year. And even though we are starved, in mourning, and on the verge of insanity, let us continue our customs and traditions of long ago. In those days, after services, we went up to our parents, our children and friends to wish them a good year. We don't know where they are now, or rather, we do know, which is worse. Let us, nevertheless, pronounce our good wishes—and leave God to transmit them to whomever they belong."

Whereupon the assembly cried out in unison and with all its might, as though wanting to shake heaven and earth: "A good year! A good year!"[2]

Through rituals we can acknowledge the sacred meaning in our life transitions. We might already use ritual to celebrate our personal passages—a birthday, a new home, a new job. Our rituals can be derived from many spiritual traditions to highlight the holiness of humanity's common milestones: birth, naming, puberty, marriage, and death. In her book *States of Grace*, Charlene Spretnak describes a ceremony she and her women friends created to celebrate their daughters' menarche:

On Saturday afternoon the mothers prepare an altar…a cloth on which they set red candles and a pot of…red daisies, along with Goddess figurines, pine cones, an abalone shell filled with dried cypress needles, and other favorite objects.… We invoke the presence of the four directions.… We tell the girls about some of the many, many cultural responses to menses as a visitation of transformative power, a sacred time set apart from the mundane…. Then, one by one, the women tell the story of their menarche…the excitement, the embarrassment, the confusion, the family's response. After each story, the speaker receives a crescent moon painted…on her forehead…. The circle is filled with laughter and tears, blessings and hope.[3]

To enjoy the benefits of ritual, many people will have to grapple with effects of earlier experiences. Luckily, most of us have at least some positive history with ritual that gives us a foundation for our unique rituals.

A HISTORY OF RITUAL

Whether or not we participated in rituals when we were children, ritual is already woven into our lives, though we may not always be aware of it.

THE FIRST RITUALS

The daily routines of being fed, comforted, bathed, dressed, and helped to sleep were our first rituals. Being cared for in a timely and consistent fashion as infants gave us a sense of connection to other humans. Through these rituals, we learned to trust that our needs would be met and all was well.[4]

Unfortunately, parental neglect, abuse, mental illness, or addiction often cheats children of the security these rituals give. People subjected to deprivation like this as very young children may face major challenges when they attempt to incorporate ritual into their lives. If this was your experience, establishing daily rituals for eating, sleeping, working, and relating to other people will be the foundation for more explicitly "spiritual" rituals. I encourage you to make a commitment to building daily rituals as an important part of your spiritual path.

Make a few notes about rituals from your early childhood. ✍

RITUAL INSIDE THE FAMILY AND RELIGIOUS SETTINGS

During our preschool and school-age years, our rituals were more reciprocal—we both created them and took part in them. We learned to engage with others both inside and outside our families in carrying out ritual. We were participating in rituals when we played peekaboo, "house," and "church." Here, a woman describes a ritual passed from generation to generation in her family, one that taught her about her family relationships:

> My father had a bedtime story that he would tell me when I was upset about something. It was about being out in this warm, cozy little house in the woods on a very cold night. Everybody's under a great big comforter. Outside it's cold but inside the house it's warm and safe. I think his mother told him that story, and he told it to me. It was a ritual between him and me. I loved it.

When I was a child, I lived near a neighborhood in which flowering crab apple trees were planted on every boulevard for blocks and blocks. Each spring on the way home from church we would drive slowly along the curving streets, enjoying the cloudlike splashes of deep pink and the light, sweet fragrance of the blossoms. This family ritual filled me with a sense of grace, wonder, and connection to the natural world.

During elementary school, most of us had some experience of religious ritual at weekly worship services, baptisms, weddings, or funerals. At that time, these rituals probably seemed complex; it was difficult to understand their meaning. Since we don't usually develop the ability to think symbolically until adolescence, much of the core meaning of religious rituals may have been lost on us. We may have found these rituals dull and meaningless.

On the other hand, maybe we did feel strongly connected to the sacred through worship services. Both Lee and Karen were raised in the Catholic church, but they experienced the Mass in dramatically different ways:

> LEE: I got very bored in church. The sermons weren't con-
> nected to my life at all. I heard about raising money, becom-

ing a nun or a priest. I heard about doctrine that meant nothing to me. Nothing from church seemed to carry over at home or at school.

KAREN: Everything being in Latin made me feel kind of mystical. I loved the rituals—the votive candles, the bells, the incense. I just kind of felt holy and special in the church.

Some families practice religious rituals at home. We may have said grace or bedtime prayers, prayed the Rosary, or taken part in Shabbat meals. Ideally, these help us feel a link to the divine through our human community. In her memoir, *Deborah, Golda and Me*, Letty Cottin Pogrebin captured all the sensual and relational details of her family's celebration of Passover:

> Passover always reminds me of my mother…. I remember how efficiently she unearthed her Passover recipe files…to double-check the traditional recipes for gefilte fish, chopped liver, chicken soup with matzo balls, potato pudding, carrot tzimmes, macaroons—all of which she would make from scratch…. To this day, I can remember the look of our seder table: the damask cloth with dim pink shadows from red-wine spills of meals past; the ceremonial plate with separate compartments for the parsley, *haroset*, gnarled horseradish root, roasted shank bone, and charred hard-boiled egg; the cut-glass bowls for salt water; three matzot in their layered satin case; two pair of candlesticks, chrome and brass; the silver goblet for the Prophet Elijah.[5]

In troubled families, some rituals are practiced, but often not consistently. For example, an alcoholic father may lead grace at mealtimes only when he is sober. A severely depressed mother may read her children a bedtime story and tuck them into bed only on her "good" days. The daughter of an alcoholic mother describes her childhood experience of ritual:

I counted on my mother to be the creator and preserver of holidays because other mothers were doing it. But when she was drinking, I couldn't depend on anything. I never knew from year to year whether we'd pull off Thanksgiving dinner. I couldn't say for sure that we were going to have a turkey or that it would be completely cooked. So I learned not to count on family ritual. It might happen or it might not. It wasn't all that meaningful for me because it was never secure.

As a result of such unpredictable ritual practices in childhood, you may be skeptical about the role of ritual in your spiritual life now. You may express this by avoiding rituals or being cynical about them. You might feel attracted to some rituals, but take part in them only sporadically.

Abuse directly associated with ritual or worship is the most harmful. Some people are actually hit or verbally abused on the way to services; others are humiliated or beaten because they didn't perform some religious ritual perfectly, like a First Communion. Some people are abused in a ritualistic fashion. For instance, you might have been awakened in the middle of the night for religious harangues, required to pray on your knees for hours at a time, or systematically starved "to make you more holy." In extreme circumstances people are even raped, tortured, or terrorized during satanic rites or other ritual abuse.

Such damaging experiences make rituals extraordinarily difficult now. You may find yourself flooded with painful memories and feelings when you take part. You may feel stark terror at the thought of entering a place of worship, or physically ill when you see a votive candle or smell incense. You may be able to participate in rituals only by switching off your feelings.

If you associate rituals with abuse or violation, anything you do to heal your childhood wounds will help clear the way for better relationships with yourself, others, and your spiritual life.

Make a few brief notes about memories of ritual at home or church. ✍

RITUALS AWAY FROM HOME OR CHURCH

For some of us, the impact of inconsistent or painful childhood experiences of ritual in family or religious settings was softened by our participation in rituals outside of them.

For example, I went to the same Girl Scout camp every summer for eight years. There were rituals for nearly everything we did at camp, but the one I remember most clearly was the dishwashing ritual. After every meal, the cooks delivered three large, shallow pans of water—one soapy, one hot and clear, and one hot with bleach in it—to each of the twenty or so tables in the dining room. Working in a line, we passed each dish and utensil through the three stations. Then we dried them and carried them in stacks back to the high cupboards on the wall.

All the while we sang together—a whole dining room full of kids of all ages, along with the adults. Some of the songs were in other languages. There were rounds and spirituals. I remember cowboy songs. Some were just for fun, but most of them carried inspiring or nurturing messages.

Participating year after year, I felt connected to all the girls who had sung these songs before me—girls from other times, other countries, and other races. I felt connected to my own history and memories of previous years at camp. Many songs were about the beauty of creation and our place in it, so I felt connected to nature and to God.

Many of us were inspired and deeply touched by experiences like these. We can now count on them to act as an inner guide as we begin to explore the role of ritual for us now. ✍

EXPERIENCES OF RITUAL IN ADULTHOOD

The effects of abuse and neglect or other childhood pain don't always disappear when we grow up. They continue to color our thoughts, feelings, and actions.

Unconsciously living out the effects of your history, you may have joined a religious community whose worship included sermons that eroded your fragile self-esteem by stressing your sinfulness, or compromised your relationship with God by emphasizing God's wrath. Or you may have participated in a community where participation in ritual hinged on the leader's capricious judgment of the "goodness" of your conduct.

Understandably, you may have chosen an emotionally abusive partner who uses scorn or the "silent treatment" to keep you from taking part in rituals. Some people have violent partners who force them to participate in rituals against their will, or forcefully keep them from going to church. A woman now in her sixties tells of her husband's abuse and the effect on her church attendance:

> My marriage to Allen [in the 1940s] caused a pretty big scandal. I was Catholic and he was Methodist. We were married in the Catholic church, and he promised to raise our children as Catholics.
>
> At first, everything was fine. I went to church alone every Sunday, but that was no problem for me. Our first son, Andy, was baptized Catholic. After that, Allen started drinking more. On Sundays he would be hung over and if Andy had a cold or something, Allen didn't want to get up and care for him while I went to church. I stayed home a couple of times, but I felt terrible about missing church.
>
> From there it gradually got worse. First he would want to have sex on Sundays and that would make me late for church. Then he started complaining and criticizing me for going to church. He escalated to ridiculing my religion and the priest. All this time I was still going to church most Sundays.
>
> When none of this worked, he really turned ugly. He would block the door and threaten to lock me out if I went to church. Once he did lock me out and I had to go to my mother's with the kids. I really was frightened for our safety. Eventually, I stopped going to church. I didn't set foot in a church except for a wedding or a funeral for the next thirty years, until Allen died.

Sometimes we are excluded from rituals not because of parental or spousal abuse, but because of beliefs or prejudices of a religious group.

For example, women (as well as gay men, lesbians, bisexuals, and transgender people) are excluded from key roles by many Christian denominations and by Orthodox Judaism. The following story, related by Letty Cottin Pogrebin, captures the pain of this:

> When E. M. Broner lost her father, she wanted to spend eleven months saying Kaddish for him. Reform synagogues *would* count her in the minyan but they do not have daily services; an Orthodox shul has daily services but would not count her in the minyan. What a choice: to honor her father she had to dishonor herself. At an old Orthodox synagogue on West 23rd Street, where she was the only woman in the dwindling congregation, she conducted a war of nerves with ten angry men who kept trying to entomb her behind a *mehitzah* made of heavy drapes and opaque shower curtains. In their zeal to block her body from their view and her voice from their ears, they cared not at all if they obliterated *her* sight and hearing so that even her passive witness to the service would be impossible.[6]

If you wish, make a few notes about your significant adulthood experiences of ritual. ✍

Not surprisingly, our past encounters with ritual shape our present expectations. For example, if we were ritualistically violated, ritual may seem to be a trap. If we were sexually abused by the clergy, we may expect betrayal if we participate in worship services. If our family's rituals were not consistent, we may be afraid to trust others in these settings now. Consequently, you will probably need to revisit some of your painful experiences to clear your path and enjoy rituals in the future.

If we were lucky enough to have been consoled by rituals in the past, we may turn to them trustingly when we are troubled. If singing in church or synagogue gave you a sense of belonging when you were growing up, you may expect to feel solidarity in ritual experiences now.

FOSTERING YOUR USE OF RITUAL

Even though you may wish to avoid ritual or deny the value of it, it will creep into your life at some point anyway. For example, you may create personal rituals, such as reading meditation books every morning or night. You may enjoy the simple ritual of a Twelve Step meeting and realize that other rituals seem less threatening than before or that they even become appealing. Or as your spirituality deepens through prayer or meditation and a community relationship, you may take part in rituals or worship services without even thinking twice.

Even as some of the obstacles to ritual fall away, you may find that using rituals involves significant challenges.

THE CHALLENGES

The first challenge will be to ensure your safety and well-being. Understandably, in your intense desire to be healed and get on with your life, you may force yourself to experiment with ritual without taking into account any vulnerability you may have. You will need to pace your exploration so that you protect yourself from the pain of being thrown off-center. Self-care will keep you true to yourself. You won't act precipitously or withdraw from yourself or others. You can always leave a situation in which your emotions are so strong that you can't think clearly or make sound decisions. You can take a break while you restore inner equilibrium. Take all the time you need to understand your feelings about a ritual before you go on to another.

Once you trust your ability to stay safe, you can move to the second challenge: learning to note your responses, emotional and intellectual, without having to act on them. Every aspect of an experience of ritual is rich with information to deepen self-knowledge. And self-knowledge allows you to select experiences that connect you more to yourself, others, and the sacred. Becoming a self-observer enables you to shift from reacting to choosing. Then you can sort out the elements of your response, distinguishing between thoughts and feelings and between past and present.

Your third challenge is to shape your exploration of rituals around your deepest and most compassionate understanding of yourself. From this place, you'll know what you are ready to pursue. You can choose not to explore ritual if it doesn't feel authentic. You can go at your own pace and trust yourself to know what works for you and what doesn't. You can even decide this is not a good time to tackle ritual.

AVENUES FOR EXPLORATION

There are many ways to gain deeper understanding of your relationship with ritual. Each of the following offers slightly different insights. Some will be more useful than others. As you read, be aware of your thoughts, feelings, and memories. Be alert to what attracts or intrigues you, what repels or frightens you. Your reactions give important clues about what will suit you.

Look at your past and present involvement with religious and spiritual rituals. Despite the fact that ritual is everywhere in the human community, few of us have examined it systematically. One way to do this is to write in your journal about your memories of ritual or worship. If you do this, you may find that your feelings about rituals change.

Explore your current rituals. You probably engage in many rituals, things you repeatedly do at a certain time each day or during certain seasons. Whether explicitly spiritual or not, these practices usually have more meaning than what is on the surface. These might be family rituals or come from your relationships with friends or a spouse, or you may have some of your very own. For example, you may have created a reading and writing ritual around your spiritual journey and this book. Maybe it's a yoga or t'ai chi practice. Preparing special foods for special occasions is certainly a ritual. So is hunting or fishing every year. And so is regularly visiting a public garden, museum, art gallery, or anyplace else.

Dialogue about ritual. Talk with others about experiences of ritual—theirs and yours—and write about it in your journal. For example, you might want to ask someone how he or she is currently involved in ritual and what meaning it holds. Or you might want to talk over childhood experiences with a friend or family member. Or you might want to ask a recovering person who seems comfortable with ritual to talk to you about his or her journey.

Imagine participating in various rituals. You can gain a deeper understanding about ritual by mentally trying out different possibilities. For example, you might envision being in a worship setting from childhood, a contemporary church or temple service, or a nontraditional spiritual ritual, such as a solstice gathering.

Begin by imagining yourself approaching the ritual space. As you do, notice how you're feeling, what you're thinking, and what you want. Try to observe your reaction carefully without being swept away by it. You may find it helpful to write as you visualize the situation. With each new thought, feeling, or impulse, see if you can go a little deeper. What memories or feelings underlie your reaction? What is the source of your reaction? What does it tell you about what you need? What you need to avoid? Let this process take you wherever you need it to. Take whatever time (even weeks or months) you need to understand your reactions fully.

Experiment with ritual. The purpose of experimenting is to gain clarity. First, you will learn more about your vulnerabilities and needs. Second, you will learn which rituals help you to make the best connections with yourself, your communities, and your Higher Power.

You might decide to say a prayer each morning and evening. You might decide to attend a church or synagogue service or a solstice ritual. The opportunity to attend a baptism, bris, wedding, or funeral can be part of your exploration. Experiment freely, feeling no obligation to make a commitment.

Consider involving others in your process. Maybe you'd like to ask someone to come along when you attend a service. You could talk about the experience afterward.

As you participate in the ritual, notice what touches you, opens your spirit. Notice what you dislike. What makes you close down or mentally go away? Notice what you remembered later. Why was it memorable? Take the time to understand your reactions. Discussing your experience with trusted friends might be helpful.

Enter into your process. When you pay attention to any aspect of your spiritual life, it begins to change. It seems to take on a life of its own, carrying you like a gentle current toward new ideas and practices. You may find yourself paddling against the current of ritual in your life, frightened of being carried to a place of oppression, abuse, or terror. If so, you can drop anchor to slow yourself down and focus on making yourself safe. Spiritual growth does not require that you be emotionally overwhelmed.

It may be that your resistance to ritual is rooted not in terror, but in needing to be in control. Take an honest look within. You may find that your opposition isn't as much of a problem as you first thought. On your present spiritual path you may have already experienced healing that comes from surrendering to the flow of the sacred.

Your relationship with ritual will evolve throughout your life. At times it may recede into the background. At other times it may be a struggle, demanding an emotional investment from you. If you cultivate your use of ritual through good times and bad, it will bring vitality to your spiritual life.

The exercises in the Exploration and Discovery section will help you begin a relationship with ritual by discovering more about your history with it. Take a few minutes now to look over the exercises and decide which one you would like to do first. When you are ready, turn to the Passageway exercise.

PASSAGEWAY

Take a few minutes to relax and settle yourself. When you're ready, begin.

Focus on your breathing, breathing in and breathing out. 🌿 Notice the air moving in 🌿 and out of your nose. 🌿 Be aware of the rising and falling of your abdomen as you breathe in 🌿 and out 🌿 in 🌿 and out. 🌿

When you're ready, 🌿 let your weight settle completely onto the floor or the chair. 🌿 Relax all your muscles 🌿 and let the floor or the chair hold you up. 🍃 Just let yourself relax and be completely supported. 🍃 Relax your shoulders 🍃 your arms 🍃 your back 🍃 your hips 🍃 your legs. 🍃

Now use your imagination to create a scene in which you are on a long hike and you are tired 🍃 and hot 🍃 and thirsty. 🍃 Imagine the setting in detail. 🍃 Be aware of what you see when you look around 🍃 the time of day 🍃 the season 🍃 the weather 🍃 what you hear 🍃 what you smell. 🍃

Now imagine yourself coming upon a small pool of clear, pure, cool spring water. 🍃 Let yourself see the pool and what surrounds it 🍃 the shape of the land, the soil, the plants, the trees. 🍃 Now come closer to the pool and look down. 🍃 See its gently sloping sides 🍃 like a graceful bowl. 🍃 See how clear the water is 🍃 how perfectly it reflects the sky and the other surroundings 🍃 like a mirror. 🍃

Put your hands in the water. 🍃 Feel the coolness of the water on your hands. 🍃 Splash some of it on your arms 🍃 your face. 🍃 Feel the water refresh you. 🍃

Now slowly step into the pool, wading only as far as you want to go. 🍃 Feel the gentle coolness of the water on your feet 🍃 your legs. 🍃 Wade in as far as you want. 🍃 Feel your skin tingling 🍃 your senses coming alive. 🍃

Cupping your hands, take a drink of the water. 🍃 Feel the water in your mouth 🍃 its purity and freshness. 🍃 When you are ready, swallow and feel it cool your throat and your stomach. 🍃 Feel the refreshing coolness slide down inside your body. 🍃 Drink as much water as you like. 🍃 Drink until your thirst is satisfied. 🍃 Feel the water refresh your body 🍃 and your spirit. 🍃 Feel the cool, fresh, pure spring water restoring your body 🍃 and your spirit. 🍃

173

When you're ready, slowly wade out of the pool. ❧ Take as much time as you want. ❧ Gently return to the edge of the pool. ❧ Feel the air on your damp skin, cooling you even more, ❧ refreshing you. ❧

Now, when you are ready, gently bring yourself back to the present time and place. ❧ Take whatever time you need to make the transition. ❧ Take a few minutes to reorient yourself and stretch your body a bit.

Exploration and Discovery

In this section you will explore some of your experiences of ritual. You may find that you have many emotions as you tell your story. Since they can give you valuable information about your spiritual life, try to observe them carefully.

Exercise 1:
Revisiting a Ritual from Childhood

Turn to a new page in your journal. Give yourself a few minutes to call to mind a family or religious ritual from your childhood.

1. *Tell the story of what happened.* Include as many details as you can. Use the following questions to guide you, but do not let them limit you. ✐

   • What was the sequence of events? When did it take place—what season, what time of day? How old were you? Where did it take place? Who was present? What were you wearing? What did you see? Hear? Smell? Taste? What were your feelings during this experience? After it?

   Take a few minutes to read over what you've written. Be aware of your feelings as you do. If any more details come to mind, write them down. ✐

2. *Recenter yourself.* If you find that you're tired or unfocused, consider taking a short break or returning to the Passageway exercise
   for a few minutes.

3. *Reflect on the experience.* ✍

   - How was the ritual important to you? What did it mean to you?
     What messages did it give you about your relationships with the
     sacred or with other people?
   - How, if at all, did this ritual nurture you? Harm you?
   - How does this experience affect your spiritual life now?

4. *If you wish, explore two or three more rituals using the same format.*

EXERCISE 2:
EXPLORING AN ADULTHOOD RITUAL EXPERIENCE

Turn to a new page in your journal. Take a few minutes to call to mind
the spiritual or religious rituals you have participated in as an adult.
Choose one that was particularly meaningful to you—one where you felt
your connection with the sacred.

1. *Tell the story of what happened.* Include as many details as you can,
   using the following questions as guides. ✍

   - What was the sequence of events? When did it take place—what
     season, what time of day? How old were you? Where did it take
     place? Who was present? What were you wearing? What did
     you see? Hear? Smell? Taste? What were your feelings during this
     ritual? After it?
   - Describe the parts of the ritual that particularly touched your
     heart or echoed your story. What was especially meaningful to
     you?

2. *Recenter yourself.*

3. *Reflect on the experience.* How has this experience influenced your spiritual journey? Describe its effect as fully as you can. ✍

4. *If you wish, explore two or three more rituals using the same format.* You may wish to write about an experience that was painful for you.

Feel free to take a break at this point. Let what you have learned from your reading and writing simmer for a while.

EXERCISE 3:
INVESTIGATING YOUR CURRENT RITUALS

Turn to a new page in your journal. Quickly, without stopping to think, write down as many of your personal rituals as you can. Include anything you do again and again in the same way. Don't rule out activities because they are embarrassing or seem trivial. Include rituals of daily life, seasonal rituals, rituals that are specifically spiritual or religious, and others that aren't. If you reach a stopping point, sit quietly and wait for other rituals to come to mind. List them quickly without evaluating them.

When your list is as complete as you can make it, read it over. Choose one or two rituals to explore more intensively. For each, answer some or all of the following questions: ✍

- What do you enjoy about this ritual? What do you dislike?
- Does it have any meaning for you? If so, what is it? If not, what or who is keeping it in your life?
- How does it connect you more deeply to yourself? To others? To the sacred? Be as specific as you can.
- How does it cut you off from yourself? From others? From the sacred? Be specific.
- How does this ritual contribute to your healing or recovery? Interfere with it?
- Is there anything you would like to change about the way you do this ritual? Make a note of it.

REFLECTION AND INTEGRATION

When you're ready, take the time to review everything you've written as you read this chapter. As you do, be aware of your feelings and make a note of them. You may find you have a number of different emotions. Be attentive to any new insights or questions that may surface. It may be of value to write your responses to these questions: ✍

- What patterns do you see in your relationship with ritual over the course of your life? Describe them.
- What elements in ritual experiences have particularly moved or touched you? What are the qualities of rituals that you especially enjoy?
- How has ritual been a difficult or painful element in your spiritual life? A life-giving or joyful one?
- In your history with ritual, are there experiences that have wounded you? Describe them and how they affect your spiritual life at present.
- Have you had experiences with ritual that could function as a foundation for new exploration? Describe them.
- What role does ritual play in your healing or recovery at the present time?
- What might be your next step(s) in connection with ritual?

REFERENCES

1. Linda Hogan, "All My Relations," *Parabola* 17 (Spring 1992):34-35.
2. Elie Wiesel, *One Generation After* (New York: Random House, 1970), 184-186.
3. Charlene Spretnak, *States of Grace* (San Francisco: HarperSanFrancisco, 1991), 146-47.
4. Erik Erikson, *Toys and Reasons: Stages in the Ritualization of Experience* (New York: W.W. Norton, 1977), 85-118.
5. Letty Cottin Pogrebin, *Deborah, Golda and Me: Being Female and Jewish in America* (New York: Crown, 1991), 17-18.
6. Pogrebin, 51-52.

10.

FILLING UP AND SPILLING OVER:
COMPASSION AND SERVICE

*The spiritual life...is not achieved by denying one part of
life for the sake of another. The spiritual life is achieved
only by listening to all of life and learning to respond to
each of its dimensions wholly and with integrity.*
—*Joan D. Chittister, OSB,* Wisdom Distilled from the Daily

*If I am not for myself, who will be? If I am for myself alone,
who am I? If not now, when?*

—*Hillel*

*I*n all enduring spiritual traditions, it is a given that compassion and
service are an integral part of walking a spiritual path. Both oral and
written traditions challenge people of faith to welcome strangers; to care
for the poor, the vulnerable, the downhearted; and to create just and lib-
erating systems in society.

Often compassion and service are the natural overflow of being filled
up in our relationship with the divine. Through prayer, we become connected to the wisdom and energy of our Higher Power. Through community, we are encouraged, taught, and nourished by others. As we
understand more about the link between our well-being and the well-
being of the human community and the earth, acts of compassion may
come naturally to us.

Sometimes, though, something interrupts this process. We may feel
drawn to service but somehow never quite follow through. We may begin
volunteering at a soup kitchen or food shelf, and then drift away. We may

179

throw ourselves headlong into a community project, only to burn out and quit in exhaustion.

If something like this has happened to you, you probably felt ashamed or guilty. You may have wondered what was wrong with you or accused yourself of being selfish. You may have compared yourself negatively with others who gave more.

BLOCKS TO COMPASSION AND SERVICE

Impasses like this are not the result of character flaws. Instead, they happen because for some reason we are not filling up—or, though we are being filled, our inner resources are also being drained so that there is no overflow.

WHAT KEEPS US FROM FILLING UP?

Compassion and service are built on empathy, that sense of emotional attunement that tells us what we can afford to give, and what others might need. Empathy is learned in childhood from our experiences of being treated compassionately by our parents and other adults. Unfortunately, in some families empathy for children is intermittent or absent. When parents lack empathy, their children grow up without compassion for themselves.

If your history was like this, you may deny or repress your needs. If they surface unexpectedly, you may criticize yourself for having them. You may pride yourself on being self-sufficient or emotionally untouchable. However, your unmet needs probably leave you feeling empty or hungry for the care of others, so what you are able to give may end up feeling draining rather than fulfilling. Therefore it may be difficult to sustain.

We fill up emotionally when we receive care from other people. But if our history has been short on empathy, this can be difficult. Parental empathy is the mirror that shows us we are lovable and valuable. Without it, we can grow up feeling unimportant to others and undeserving of their love. As adults we may not even recognize the fact that someone is interested in our well-being. We may not believe that anyone could care about us in a dependable way. We may not know how to "let caring in."

Without being able to receive love and compassion, it is hard to replenish yourself when you give service, and so your giving may be very difficult to sustain. As you cultivate empathy for yourself and learn how to receive from others, you will notice a new sense of spontaneous generosity. ✐

WHAT DRAINS US?

Many of us have learned in our religious upbringing that service has to involve sacrifice. We may have been taught that service which does not cut to the bone, whether emotionally or financially, does not go far enough. A friend expressed it to me this way:

> I struggle a lot with a stereotypical notion of service, one probably based on a too-literal interpretation of the Gospel sometime in the dim past. The ideal is that the only service that "counts" is service to the poor, the needy, the dying, the lonely—the truly down-and-out folks. And service only counts if it is done at great personal sacrifice. Things that involve getting paid don't count, of course. Service should be done without regard to my own well-being. With this ideal in mind, I never measure up. I feel constantly guilty that I am not doing more.

Religious scriptures and dogmas are often the source of this ethos of self-surrender. For example, the Judeo-Christian tradition centers around those who were chosen by God and who totally surrendered their lives to God's service—Abraham, Moses, the Old Testament prophets, Jesus, and Jesus' disciples.

If you were raised in a troubled family, you may be particularly susceptible to the gnawing feeling that you could—and should—always do more for others. In your family experience, your well-being may have been sacrificed to protect your parents' drinking, conceal their mental illness, preserve their toxic marriage, or hide their sexual abuse.

In a situation like this, children learn to sacrifice their needs to survive.

181

They do not develop an inner radar to tell them that certain demands by others for attention, concern, or effort are excessive. Because they do not learn how to set limits, as adults they may feel drained by others' needs.

If this is your story, you may have an unconscious habit of violating your own needs in order to be of service to others. You may exhaust yourself rather than let anyone else down. You may feel terribly guilty if you say no when someone needs your help.

If your family was frequently in crisis, you probably learned to give what was needed at the moment as best you could. What was needed may not have been what you would most authentically give. Consequently, as an adult you may not know much about your unique gifts and talents, so your service may be guided more by "shoulds" than by the promptings of your heart. Often we experience this kind of service as draining, whereas sharing our natural talents renews our spirit. ✍

Cultivating Compassion and Service:
A Framework for Spiritual Healing

The word "compassion," in its original sense, means "to suffer with." Thus, compassion involves our entering into a relationship with someone in a unique situation because we understand what is needed and reach out to help. Because it is a deeply personal response to unique circumstances, an authentic act of compassionate service is unrepeatable. It cannot be fully planned and its outcome cannot be fully predicted.

Truly compassionate service—whether we are giver or receiver—happens when we are moved by the sacred within and around us. It is not so much something we do or receive but something we are blessed with. We recognize that we are taking part in a sacred cycle of caring and healing, simultaneously giving and being given to, helping and being helped, caring and being cared for, healing and being made whole.

One woman told me about an event in her life that shows the circular and uplifting character of compassionate service:

> I was driving home on a country road on a bitterly cold, windy winter day. I saw a car that had gone off the road. The

driver was outside trying to figure out what he could do. He was dressed in a very light coat and wore no hat or gloves. I knew it was at least five miles to the nearest phone.

It was clear he needed help—he was in danger and didn't seem to know it. I always carry a towing chain in the car and I thought I could pull him out, so I stopped. We hooked the chain to both cars, and after several attempts, we finally got his car back on the road.

Then we stood there, two strangers face to face, between the two cars, in that horrible wind. Very solemnly, almost as in a ritual, we introduced ourselves and shook hands. Only then did I realize he was from another country—his English was broken. Then we parted, kind of awkwardly.

When I started out again, I felt a tremendous feeling of love surrounding me, like a cloud of light. Everything looked extraordinarily clear and beautiful to me for several minutes. I felt somehow that I was at the very center of what was important in the world.

Cultivating compassion requires us to take radical steps; each involves a choice not to reenact any negative patterns from our past. Our goal is to move from self-neglect to self-care, from caretaking to compassionate service.

WE GROUND OURSELVES IN THE SACRED

True compassion springs not from our will but from our relationship with the sacred. By its very nature, our spirituality expresses itself in some form of service to others. If we are straining to be compassionate because we think we should be, it is not real caring. Our compassion grows out of our listening for the subtle complexities of events. We can practice listening by setting aside time for solitude and reflection, prayer or meditation.

One woman shared her insight about this process:

For lots and lots of years, I was doing all the "Christian

things"—bringing over food when someone died, for example—out of a sense of duty or obedience to an abstract belief rather than from being in tune with the spirit. I find that if I can just get in tune with the spirit, then the right kind of service comes naturally.

Over time, our prayer or meditation practices teach us to wait for the right time and the best way to offer our care to others. Waiting brings us deeper into relationship with the truth of the situation. This truth tells us what, if anything, is needed from us.

Through our participation in ritual and a spiritual community, we are exposed to different ways of caring shaped by many spiritual traditions. We learn about our true place in the universe and the human community.

WE LEARN TO CARE FOR OURSELVES FIRST

Making ourselves the primary beneficiary of our compassion and service is possible only if we foster a relationship of hospitality with any parts of ourselves that we have disowned. We need to listen to our feelings, our needs, our longings, our dreams. When we treat ourselves with compassion, we come to know ourselves very deeply and fully. We learn to face our faults and our mistakes with kindness. We learn to accept ourselves as we are, not as we could or should be.

Aware of our own process, we become more closely attuned to our state of emptiness or fullness, our state of shame or self-affirmation, our state of pain or healing. Given this awareness, we gradually learn to make moment-to-moment decisions when we encounter situations that call for compassion and service.

It is a bold step to put ourselves first in line to receive our own compassion. Others may see us as selfish or self-absorbed, but we understand that self-care is a means to an end: We care for ourselves so we can be of service to others.

Learning to care for ourselves first is like slowly filling a large container drop by drop, until our self-acceptance overflows and touches others. If our container is completely empty, we may need months or years to fill it.

WE DO NOT FORCE OURSELVES

Sue Monk Kidd, in her essay "Birthing Compassion," writes about her encounter (as a twelve-year-old) with an old woman in a nursing home:

> My mother had not heard my pleas that I be spared the unjust sentence of visiting a nursing home when my friends were enjoying the last day of summer vacation at the...pool. Smarting from the inequity, I stood before this ancient-looking woman, holding a bouquet of crepe paper flowers. Everything about her saddened me—the worn-down face, the lopsided grin, the tendrils of gray hair protruding from a crocheted lavender cap. I thrust the bouquet at her. She looked at me, a look that pierced me to the marrow of my...bones. Then she spoke [these] words: "You didn't want to come, did you, child?"
>
> "Oh yes, I wanted to come," I protested.
>
> A smile lifted one side of her mouth.
>
> "It's okay," she said. "You can't force the heart."[1]

It is second nature to many of us to "force our heart." However, when we do, we do violence to our spirit. To find a sustainable path to service, we need to decide not to force ourselves to care or to serve when we are not ready. This decision requires courage, because it may stir up our shame, guilt, or fear about being judged "selfish." It may bring some of us face-to-face with our belief that if we fail to meet the needs of others, they will stop caring about us.

WE CUT THE LINK BETWEEN SACRIFICE AND SERVICE

Our compassion is more authentic when we understand the difference between sacrifice and service. Compassionate service rarely involves a life-consuming mission. Instead, opportunities are found in our ordinary life experiences. For example, you could make room to let someone change lanes in front of you, open a door for someone whose arms are full, help a friend start a stalled car, or smile and greet a stranger. You might spend a little extra time with a child who is frightened about going to a new school, or take a few minutes to listen to a friend who is upset.

When we serve out of a sense of relationship, our actions naturally flow out of who we understand ourselves to be and what we have to offer. Enjoying what we are doing, we feel connected to ourselves, to others, and to the sacred. We feel enriched by the experience.

Fred Means, in an interview with Phillip L. Berman, told the story of his effort to save a woman's life by collecting money for the operation she needed and browbeating a hospital administrator into authorizing her admission—this despite the fact that he himself was seriously ill and jobless. When Means succeeded, he reported:

> [I] had the greatest feelin'. There's no way to describe it. But God...I just felt his presence. It just seemed like he wrapped me in a mantle or somethin'. Words won't describe how I felt. I had the greatest feelin' I ever had in all of my life.[2]

Resentment is a signal that our service has become contaminated by sacrifice, to the detriment of everyone involved. A woman I interviewed described the attitudes she discovered in herself many years ago when she was working with the homeless:

> I thought of my work with the homeless as sacrificing. I would sacrifice for them. But if they made a lot of noise or messed up the place, I would become resentful and demanding. Now when I find myself thinking that way, I know I'm not in a healthy place.

We need to distinguish between fixing and caring. Simply *being with* someone in need, whether or not we can do something tangible, affirms the healing power of listening and being emotionally present. In her memoir *Virgin Time* Patricia Hampl described the ethos of care displayed by St. Francis of Assisi:

Francis ran first to find the lepers. He didn't run howling into the woods to *help* them. He wasn't a do-gooder, not a missionary in the convert-the-heathen sort of way....

This suffering-with/being-with creates a ground of equality missing from other missionary motives with their inevitable one up/one down benevolence.[3]

We Recognize and Cultivate Our Unique Gifts

Through our relationship with the sacred, we become aware of all the gifts we have to offer and the passions that activate them. When our care for others springs from these sources, we feel fully alive.

Reflecting on my own gifts, I wrote in my journal:

> The service I give through my work—both with clients and with writing—seems like what I was born to do. I think I need to hear people's stories and be part of their change and growth—and were I not to be able to have this I would suffer deeply. My soul itself would suffer.
>
> My connection to the earth and all her creatures feels equally primal, my awareness of it lifelong. The motivation for this kind of service feels at one with my personality and my life. Again, I think I would starve or wither if I could not help living beings to thrive.

To increase our capacity for compassion and service, we can cultivate our gifts and share them with others. You may have hands-on talents: You may shovel someone's driveway, prepare food for a friend or neighbor who is ill, or teach a child how to use tools safely. Many people have a natural aptitude for giving emotional support: You could visit someone who is housebound or volunteer as a Big Brother or Big Sister. Or you might naturally serve by praying for those suffering or in need.

Through our experiences of service, we acknowledge our interdependence with all of creation. The humility we learn helps us to be caring even when there is no concrete result or reward.

As we cultivate our gifts, we accept our limitations as well. As a friend said, "I have had to face the fact that I will never be Mother Teresa." Our honesty may bring us a measure of grief; but in the end, it frees us to develop the unique talents we do possess.

If you are ready to continue, turn to the exercises in the Exploration and Discovery section. Take a few minutes now to look them over. They are in no particular order; let your intuition guide you as you decide where to focus. When you are ready, do the Passageway exercise.

PASSAGEWAY

Begin by choosing a piece of restful music for this exercise. It should last at least twenty minutes.

Now take a brief time to settle yourself. Then turn on the music and follow these directions:

> Sit quietly with your eyes closed. Let your attention turn to the music. ❧ Relax into listening to it. ❧ Don't try to listen, but just let yourself hear what there is to hear ❧ effortlessly hearing each sound, each instrument. ❧ Hear the tune and the harmonies ❧ using only enough energy to listen. ❧

> As you listen, let the boundary between yourself and the music blur. ❧ Soften your sense of self ❧ and be at one with the sounds and the harmonies. ❧

> Now let yourself imagine others who have enjoyed this piece of music, beginning with those you know. ❧ Feel your connection to people who live in your area ❧ in other places in your country ❧ in other countries. ❧ Let the music create a ribbon that joins you with people all over the world. ❧ Let this image dwell quietly within you for a few minutes. ❧

> Return again to the music, letting it touch you in whatever way it will. ❧ Allow yourself to be at one with it in this place and time. ❧

Let your heart be open to its flow and its rhythms. 🌿

When you're ready, gently bring your attention back to the present. 🌿 Be aware of your surroundings. 🌿 Open your eyes. ✍

EXPLORATION AND DISCOVERY

The exercises in this section are designed to help you explore the theme of compassion and service. Remember to center yourself before you begin each exercise.

EXERCISE 1:
EXPLORING YOUR HISTORY WITH COMPASSION AND SERVICE

You can tell your history about compassion and service by answering some or all of the following questions. The more specific and detailed you can be, the more you will gain. ✍

1. What did you learn about compassion and service from your family?

- How were family members compassionate toward you? Not compassionate?
- How were you expected to serve and be compassionate toward members of your family?
- What were your family's values about compassion and service?
- How did family members live out—or fail to live out—these values, inside and outside the family?

2. What did you learn about compassion and service from your religious upbringing?

- What was expected of believers?
- How did you learn about this?
- How did you experience your religion's teachings? To you, were they inspiring, oppressive, loving, guilt-producing?

3. As an adult, what has been your journey in relation to compassion and service?

- What have you experimented with?
- What struggles and dilemmas have you faced? What have you resolved? What remains unsettled?

EXERCISE 2:
ASSESSING YOUR COMPASSION FOR YOURSELF

Open your journal to a new page. On the left side of it, make a list of the aspects of yourself for which you consistently feel compassion. If you prefer, you can draw them. When you finish the list, take a few minutes to relax. See whether you need to add anything.

Leaving some space in the middle of the page, use the right side to list or draw aspects of yourself for which you have no compassion or empathy. You may find it helpful to complete the sentence "I have no compassion for you when you…" for each trait. Repeat the process of resting and then adding material.

In the middle of the page, list or draw aspects of yourself for which you sometimes have compassion.

Use lines of any shape and thickness to separate the three lists.

Now take a break if you wish. When you come back, look over your responses. Notice any feelings, patterns, or conflicts. Note what you see. ✍

If you wish to explore further, you might do one of the following exercises:

- Ask yourself: If my mother or father completed this exercise about me, how would it be the same? How would it be different? If my parents completed it about themselves, how would it be the same as mine? How would it be different?
- Explore this question: If my Higher Power completed this exercise about me, how would it be the same? How would it be different?
- In your journal, interview or dialogue with one or more of the aspects on your list. ✍

EXERCISE 3:
BECOMING FAMILIAR WITH YOUR
COMPASSIONATE SELF

Turn to a new page in your journal. Choose a period of your life in which you would like to explore the compassionate part of yourself. Now, using a line drawing, collage, cut paper, or abstract design, depict your compassionate self at that time, including your feelings, dilemmas, and/or actions. Consider using your nondominant hand to make this picture. (If you prefer, write about your compassionate self at this age.)

Before you begin, you might use the following questions to focus your reflections.

- How were you expressing compassion or giving service during this period?
- Was you compassion or service blocked in any way? How?
- How well did your service match you own unique gifts? Which of your gifts (if any) were you expressing? Which remained unexpressed?
- How did you feel at the time about your efforts to serve others? Were they strained? Easy? Authentic? False? Satisfying? Guilt-producing?

When you have finished, look over the exercise. What have you discovered? How do you feel about it? If you wish, make an entry in your journal. ✍

Note: You may find it fruitful to repeat this exercise for yourself at other ages.

You will probably want to take a break at this point to allow your new insights to percolate. When you're ready, begin the Reflection and Integration section.

REFLECTION AND INTEGRATION

Take a few minutes to look over all that you've written or drawn in this chapter. Be aware of connections and patterns. Note your emotions. If you see any relationships between your reflections in this chapter and those in earlier chapters, note them as well.

In addition, you may find it useful to write your responses to some or all of the following questions: ✍

- How did your family shape your current ideas and values about compassion and service? Which experiences are helpful to you now? Which are problematic?
- How has your compassion for yourself grown? Who supports this growth?
- What are your passions and gifts? Do you usually recognize and celebrate them? Why or why not? Do you use them in the service of yourself? Of others? Why or why not?
- At this time, what is the role of compassion and service in your spiritual journey?
- Spiritually, where do you need to focus right now—on service to others or on other aspects of your spiritual life, such as prayer, community, or ritual?

REFERENCES

1. Sue Monk Kidd, "Birthing Compassion," *Weavings* (November-December 1990): 22.
2. Fred Means, "Gathered in the Dust." In *The Search for Meaning: Americans Talk About What They Believe and Why*, ed. Phillip L. Berman (New York: Ballantine Books, 1990), 303.
3. Patricia Hampl, *Virgin Time* (New York: Farrar, Straus and Giroux, 1992), 191.

11.

A Lifetime Journey:
Guides and Guidance

Just to live is holy; just to be is a blessing.
—Rabbi Abraham Joshua Heschel

Perhaps this is the most important thing for me to take back from beach-living: simply the memory that each cycle of the tide is valid, each cycle of the wave is valid, each cycle of a relationship is valid. And my shells? I can sweep them all into my pocket. They are only there to remind me that the sea recedes and returns eternally.
—Anne Morrow Lindbergh, Gift from the Sea

During college, I lived in the foothills near Boulder, Colorado. On weekends, I explored back roads and mountain trails. I vividly remember one hike to this day. Just above 10,000 feet a rough road narrows and the Arapaho Pass trail begins. Following the trail through a spruce forest, I soon emerged onto the bare sides of a mountain following the valley of tiny North Boulder Creek far below.

The trail was well-worn from the tread of countless travelers: first Arapahos, Shoshones, and Cheyennes; and later white explorers, trappers, miners, hunters, anglers, and hikers. Though I was alone, I felt their presence.

All morning I hiked up this trail, drawn by the snow-covered summit. As I reached higher altitudes, I had to stop and rest from time to time. I looked back down the valley, gaining a wider and wider view of the valley each time.

Approaching the summit, I met two men carrying large backpacks on their way down the trail. We talked for a few minutes and compared notes about the trails ahead. They told me that the trail was rough for a while just on the other side of the Divide, but it eventually turned into a four-wheel drive road. They asked where they could find water. I told them about the well in the campground and gave them each a drink from my water bottle before we parted.

Though I have never returned, that trail is clearly etched in my memory. In the last ten years, it has been a metaphor for my spiritual path. I return to it over and over in my mind as an image of the sacred journey.

In our spiritual journey, we each walk a path. In one sense, it is well-worn, like the Arapaho Pass trail; innumerable seekers have traveled the path before. Yet, it is also unique, for we each have our own departure time, pace, rest stops, and detours. We each have unique joys and learnings. And each of us appreciates different aspects of the journey and is tested in singular ways. Like me and the two backpackers, you may need help as you walk your spiritual path and companionship to revive you when your energy flags. You may need someone to point the way. You may need help removing obstacles.

Helpers and Companions for Your Journey

If your past has been painful, guides and companions may be especially important to you; without them, you might lose heart, energy, or direction in your attempt to pay attention to the holy in life. In addition to drawing energy from partners, friends, Twelve Step meetings, and religious or spiritual communities, there are two other sources of help that can be of special value: spiritual direction and psychotherapy.

Spiritual Direction

Spiritual direction has been a crucial part of my own spiritual life. Early in my own healing, it provided a sheltered, safe relationship where I could explore my images of God and develop a prayer life. At times, sessions were intense and their aftermath potent; I knew my relationship with the sacred was being reshaped with energy vastly more powerful than my own. I spent many hours talking through my paralyzing fear about being close to the sacred. Listening to myself and being heard by my spiritual director made my fear begin to subside.

Eventually, I emerged into a meadow where I could see my path clearly—not every mile of it, but certainly its form and direction. Through spiritual direction, I went from struggling to find authentic spirituality to simply living it. At that point, it was time for a different guide for the next part of my journey.

I now see spiritual direction as a trail marker for the life of my spirit. No matter how busy, preoccupied, or scattered I become, once a month I set aside a time to reflect on my spiritual life. Knowing this keeps me from getting too busy, preoccupied, or scattered. In our sessions my director and I may focus together on an encounter with the sacred, questions or struggles with prayer, a moral dilemma, or a dream. In many ways she creates an atmosphere where I can be completely present to myself and the sacred. At times she simply listens and reflects back what she's heard; at other times she guides me into deeper exploration.

Spiritual direction or guidance is a relationship where the only goal is the spiritual growth of the client (the "directee"). Despite the title, a spiritual director does not "direct," but rather facilitates and observes what already seems to be happening between a client and the sacred.

Spiritual direction provides a quiet, contemplative atmosphere in which we can put our spiritual experiences into words. It focuses not on dogma or doctrine but on our day-to-day experience of our Higher Power or what cuts us off from it. The content may include our relationships, our work, our sexuality, our decision making, our daily routine.

The best way to find a spiritual director is to ask others—friends, members of support groups, clergy. Often, retreat houses (listed in the Yellow Pages) offer spiritual direction or make referrals.

If your history includes abuse by those you should have been able to trust, you are particularly vulnerable when you enter such an important and powerful relationship. Therefore, it is a good idea to interview two or three directors (or as many as necessary) before you select one. Look until you can find someone with whom you can build a trusting relationship.

You are most likely to develop trust with a spiritual director whose personality and spiritual values are compatible with yours. Prepare for the interview by clarifying what you need and want. A qualified spiritual director has received years of extensive training. This ranges from apprenticeship with an experienced director to completion of formal instruction and supervised practice. It is a given in the tradition of the profession that spiritual directors must have their own spiritual directors as well. Ideally, they should participate in some form of consultation with other directors. (In consultation, spiritual directors discuss questions and impasses in their work with clients.) Finally, a competent and trustworthy spiritual director should keep the relationship purely professional. It is perfectly acceptable for prospective clients to ask directors about their practices and experiences in any of these areas. In fact, I strongly encourage you to do so.

PSYCHOTHERAPY

But now you understand how a history of trauma can be interwoven with every aspect of your spiritual life. If your spiritual questions or struggles are related to your history, you may find that despite your best efforts you get stuck again and again as you try to find a spiritual path. If this is the case, you might consider psychotherapy. Though it does not explicitly address spiritual healing, psychotherapy often makes spiritual growth possible because it gets back to the origins of our spiritual impasse and helps us begin to grow again.

PSYCHOTHERAPY AND SPIRITUAL DIRECTION: COMPLEMENTARY BUT SEPARATE ROLES

Spiritual direction and psychotherapy are similar and often complement each other. They also have distinct and separate roles that require different training and expertise. You might think of a psychotherapist or counselor as a guide, one who helps you formulate your goals and uses his or her skills to help you reach them. Usually, the relationship between therapist and client is intensely interpersonal. Psychotherapy is goal-oriented and time-limited.

A spiritual director is more like a naturalist than a guide. He or she can help you to be more observant in the here and now, to appreciate and wonder at the life along the path. Spiritual direction includes no expectations of change—although change certainly occurs. Therefore, there are no built-in objectives or ending times. Since the relationship between the client and a Higher Power is the focus, the relationship between director and client is intentionally kept in the background. Quite often, people benefit from seeing both a spiritual director and a therapist, even concurrently if that seems best.

HEALING SPIRITUALLY: HOW DO YOU KNOW IF YOU ARE ON AN AUTHENTIC PATH?

In the course of our spiritual journey, we can learn to recognize signs that we are on a path that will lead us into a deeper relationship with the sacred. The signs of our spiritual progress are revealed in our behavior and our beliefs about our place in the world.

CHANGES IN OUR BEHAVIOR

As we grow spiritually, we feel more connected to all parts of ourselves as well as the human community, the natural world, and the sacred as we understand it. While this sense may ebb and flow in the short run, it grows steadily when we walk an authentic spiritual path.

With our new sense of connection, we gain more trust in the process of growth, giving up our need for instant success. We develop respect for timing and become more patient with ourselves and others. Able at last to relax, we find an innate capacity for wonder, delight, and joy. We even begin to welcome and enjoy the element of surprise in our lives. We become more stable and grounded.

Released from both self-hate and overblown self-importance, we find new depths of love and generosity within, and we accept the love of others more readily. As we become more emotionally well-nourished, we are less reactive. Now our decisions and actions are consistent with our reflection and spiritual principles.

Which of these changes in behavior are already under way in your life? Make a note about them, if you wish. ✍

Changes in Our Beliefs

Healing our spiritual lives brings old false beliefs into our awareness and helps us find new beliefs and experiences. On our spiritual path we can draw on external sources of wisdom—other people, sacred scripture, the written word, prayer, and all of creation. New knowledge replaces our old belief that we are inevitably on our own, that we must find our path alone, our solutions to problems alone, our answers to troubling questions alone.

We learn that pain, which we once avoided at all costs, has the power to help us grow. We become attentive to life as it unfolds, and discover that we don't need to hold on to serenity and joy quite so tightly. We recognize the myriad ways we are connected to other people and our Higher Power, so we can let go of our need to seek spiritual perfection. We come to trust the process of spiritual growth, so we no longer need to work so hard at staying on the path.

Which of these shifts in belief have you noticed in yourself? Make a few notes, if you wish. ✍

Looking Back and Looking Ahead

As you near the end of this book, I invite you one last time to reflect on your experience—this time, from the beginning of the book to the present—and to envision what might be ahead on your spiritual path.

Your concept of spirituality has probably undergone a transformation as you have read and worked with this book. You may have begun believing that this book would help you "work on" your spirituality. You may have been looking for a "cookbook" that would establish you in a predictable spiritual life once and for all. You may have begun with a volatile mixture of fear and hope or with a lot of skepticism. Take a few minutes to recall your feelings and attitudes as you began reading this book. What attracted you to it? What were your hopes? Your questions? Your fears? If you wish, make a few notes. ✍

As you look back from your present vantage point, what do you see? What themes have recurred? What insights have emerged? What has been stirred up? What has been resolved? ✍

You have probably gained insights into what you need to travel your path and into how you feel when you provide it for yourself. You probably also know something about what you feel when you lack what you need. If you wish, make a few notes about what you have learned. ✍

In working with the chapters and exercises in this book, you have undoubtedly learned a great deal about what works for you in your spiritual life. You may experience a renewed relationship with your soul and/or with the sacred. You may have sensed a new commitment and trust in your spiritual life. You may even have a dawning awareness that a divine partner inspires your spiritual exploration. If you wish, make a few notes about the changes in your relationship with your soul and/or the sacred. ✍

You may have reached a turning point in your journey with this book, a fork in the trail where you decided to commit yourself to stay in relationship with the sacred and to continue your spiritual journey wherever it might lead you. Or you may still be exploring tentatively, getting a feel for what the process of spiritual growth involves. If you wish, make a few notes about where you stand right now in relation to your spiritual journey as a whole. ✍

Finally, I invite you to look to what lies before you. What do you see? What seems to be a natural next step? Who or what seems to offer solid guidance as you travel onward? ✍

TRAVELING YOUR PATH: A LIFELONG PROCESS

Your spiritual journey will continue as long as you live. Everything in your life has the potential to deepen your relationship with the sacred.

From the momentary sight of a butterfly or the sound of a child laughing to the dark times following a loss or serious illness, all our experiences contain the seeds of spiritual growth. Rabbi Heschel captures the essence of this when he writes, in *Quest for God*, "there is something sacred at stake in every event."

We embark on the journey to the extent that we learn to pay attention to our life and to let it teach us. All spiritual traditions recognize this fact. Some call it consciousness, some reflection, some discernment—but all point seekers toward staying awake spiritually. When we pay attention—whether by praying, journaling, completing exercises, talking with a friend or spiritual director, or participating in a retreat—something new emerges. It may be a new perspective, a new feeling, a new idea, a new insight. Awake, we are often awestruck by our inner depths or the grace suffusing us in these experiences. All that is required for spiritual growth is that we continue to pay attention.

Wherever your quest leads you, I wish you well.

Deep peace to you:
Deep peace of the running wave to you,
Deep peace of the flowing air to you,
Deep peace of the quiet earth to you,
Deep peace of the shining stars to you,
Deep peace of the gentle night to you.
Deep peace to you.
—Traditional Gaelic blessing

Selected Readings

Books

Journaling and Writing

Capacchione, Lucia. *The Creative Journal: The Art of Finding Yourself.* North Hollywood, California: Newcastle Publishing, 1989.

Goldberg, Natalie. *Writing Down the Bones: Freeing the Writer Within.* Boston: Shambhala, 1983.

Rico, Gabriele Lusser. *Writing the Natural Way.* Los Angeles: Jeremy P. Tarcher, 1983.

Solly, Richard, and Roseann Lloyd. Journey Notes: *Writing for Recovery and Spiritual Growth.* San Francisco: HarperSanFrancisco, 1989.

Images of God/Images of the Sacred

Anderson, Sherry Ruth, and Patricia Hopkins. *The Feminine Face of God: The Unfolding of the Sacred in Women.* New York: Bantam Books, 1991.

Craighead, Meinrad. *The Mother's Songs: Images of God the Mother.* New York: Paulist Press, 1986.

Mollenkott, Virginia Ramey. *The Divine Feminine: The Biblical Imagery of God as Female.* New York: Crossroad, 1984.

Ruether, Rosemary Radford. "Sexism and God-Language." In *Weaving the Visions: New Patterns in Feminist Spirituality,* edited by Judith Plaskow and Carol P. Christ.

Swidler, Leonard. *Biblical Affirmations of Woman.* Philadelphia: Westminster Press, 1979.

Prayer and Meditation

DeMello, Anthony. *Sadhana: A Way to God.* Garden City, New York: Image Books, 1984.

Edwards, Tilden. *Living in the Presence: Disciplines for the Spiritual Heart.* San Francisco: HarperSanFrancisco, 1987.

Hanh, Thich Nhat. *A Guide to Walking Meditation.* Nyack, New York: Fellowship Publications, 1985.

Hays, Edward. *Pray All Ways.* Easton, Kansas: Forest of Peace Books, 1981.

Kabat-Zinn, Jon. *Wherever You Go, There You Are.* New York: Hyperion, 1994.

Leadingham, Carrie, Joann E. Moschella, and Hilary M. Vartanian, eds. *Peace Prayers: Meditations, Affirmations, Invocations, Poems, and Prayers for Peace.* San Francisco: HarperSanFrancisco, 1992.

Levine, Stephen. *A Gradual Awakening.* Garden City, New York: Anchor Press, 1979.

Progoff, Ira. *The Practice of Process Meditation.* New York: Dialogue House, 1981.

Roberts, Elizabeth, and Elias Amidon, eds. *Earth Prayers From Around the World.* San Francisco: HarperSanFrancisco, 1991.

Ulanov, Ann, and Barry Ulanov. Primary Speech: *A Psychology of Prayer.* Atlanta: John Knox Press, 1982.

Wiederkehr, Macrina. *A Tree Full of Angels: Seeing the Holy in the Ordinary.* San Francisco: HarperSanFrancisco, 1991.

RITUAL

Ardinger, Barbara. *A Woman's Book of Rituals and Celebrations.* San Rafael, California: New World Library, 1992.

Beck, Renee, and Sydney Barbara Metrick. *The Art of Ritual.* Berkeley, California: Celestial Arts, 1990.

Imber-Black, Evan, and Janine Roberts. *Rituals for Our Times: Celebrating, Healing, and Changing Our Lives and Our Relationships.* New York: HarperCollins, 1992.

Imber-Black, Evan, Janine Roberts, and Richard Whiting, eds. *Rituals in Families and Family Therapy.* New York: W.W. Norton, 1988.

Ruether, Rosemary Radford. *Women-Church: Theology and Practice of Feminist Liturgical Communities.* San Francisco: HarperSan-Francisco, 1985.

COMPASSION AND SERVICE

Palmer, Parker J. *The Active Life: Wisdom for Work, Creativity, and Caring.* San Francisco: HarperSanFrancisco, 1990.

SPIRITUAL DEVELOPMENT AND SPIRITUAL GROWTH

Hagberg, Janet O., and Robert A. Guelich. *The Critical Journey: Stages in the Life of Faith.* Dallas: Word Publishing, 1989.

Kidd, Sue Monk. *When the Heart Waits: Spiritual Direction for Life's Sacred Questions.* San Francisco: HarperSanFrancisco, 1990.

Metzner, Ralph, Ph.D. *Opening to Inner Light: The Transformation of Human Nature and Consciousness.* Los Angeles: Jeremy P. Tarcher, 1986.

Moore, Thomas. *Care of the Soul: A Guide for Cultivating the Depth and Sacredness in Everyday Life.* New York: HarperCollins, 1992.

Schnapper, Edith B. *The Inward Odyssey: The Concept of The Way in the Great Religions of the World.* London: George Allen and Unwin, 1980.

Welch, John. *Spiritual Pilgrims: Carl Jung and Teresa of Avila.* New York: Paulist Press, 1982.

WOMEN'S SPIRITUALITY

Christ, Carol P. *Diving Deep and Surfacing: Women Writers on Spiritual Quest.* 2d ed. Boston: Beacon Press, 1986.

Gray, Elizabeth Dodson. *The Sacred Dimensions of Women's Experience.* Wellesley, Massachusetts: Roundtable Press, 1988.

Harris, Maria. *Dance of the Spirit: The Seven Steps of Women's Spirituality.* New York: Bantam Books, 1989.

Morton, Nelle. *The Journey Is Home.* Boston: Beacon Press, 1985.

Schneiders, Sandra M. "The Effects of Women's Experience on Their Spirituality." *Spirituality Today* 35 (Summer 1983):100-116.

Sewell, Marilyn, ed. *Cries of the Spirit: A Celebration of Women's Spirituality.* Boston: Beacon Press, 1991.

Vander Vort, Kay, Joan H. Timmerman, and Eleanor Lincoln, eds. *Walking in Two Worlds: Women's Spiritual Paths.* St. Cloud, Minnesota: North Star Press, 1992.

MEN'S SPIRITUALITY

Keen, Sam. *Fire in the Belly.* New York: Bantam Books, 1991.

Sellner, Edward C. *Soul-Making: The Telling of a Spiritual Journey.* Mystic, Connecticut: Twenty-Third Publications, 1991.

Solly, Richard. *Sacred Moments: Experiences of the Transcendent in the Lives of Ordinary Men.* (To be published by Hazelden in 1995.)

SPIRITUALITY OF LESBIANS AND GAY MEN

Balka, Christie, and Andy Rose, eds. *Twice Blessed: On Being Lesbian or Gay and Jewish.* Boston: Beacon Press, 1989.

Boyd, Malcolm, and Nancy L. Wilson, eds. *Amazing Grace: Stories of Lesbian and Gay Faith.* Freedom, California: Crossing Press, 1991.

Fortunato, John E. *Embracing the Exile: Healing Journeys of Gay Christians.* San Francisco: HarperSanFrancisco, 1982.

O'Neill, Craig, and Kathleen Ritter. *Coming Out Within: Stages of Spiritual Awakening for Lesbians and Gay Men.* San Francisco: HarperSanFrancisco, 1992.

Zanotti, Barbara, ed. *A Faith of One's Own: Explorations by Catholic Lesbians.* Freedom, California: Crossing Press, 1986.

SPIRITUAL DIRECTION

Fischer, Kathleen. *Women at the Well: Feminist Perspectives on Spiritual Direction.* New York: Paulist Press, 1988.

Guenther, Margaret. *Holy Listening: The Art of Spiritual Direction.* Cambridge, Massachusetts: Cowley Publications, 1992.

May, Gerald G. *Care of Mind/Care of Spirit: Psychiatric Dimensions of Spiritual Direction.* San Francisco: Harper & Row, 1982.

ABUSE AND RECOVERY

Bass, Ellen, and Laura Davis. *The Courage to Heal: A Guide for Women Survivors of Child Sexual Abuse.* New York: HarperCollins, 1988.

Cameron, Julia. *The Artist's Way: A Spiritual Path to Higher Creativity.* Los Angeles: Jeremy P. Tarcher/Perigee, 1992.

Davis, Laura. *The Courage to Heal Workbook: For Men and Women Survivors of Child Sexual Abuse.* New York: HarperCollins, 1990.

Fredrickson, Renee. *Repressed Memories: A Journey to Recovery from Sexual Abuse.* New York: Simon and Schuster, 1992.

Gil, Eliana. *Outgrowing the Pain.* New York: Dell, 1988.

Greven, Philip. *Spare the Child: The Religious Roots of Punishment and the Psychological Impact of Physical Abuse.* New York: Vintage Books, 1990.

Herman, Judith Lewis. *Trauma and Recovery.* New York: Basic Books, 1992.

Miller, Alice. *The Drama of the Gifted Child.* New York: Basic Books, 1983.

Nestingen, Signe L., and Laurel Ruth Lewis. *Growing Beyond Abuse: A Workbook for Survivors of Sexual Exploitation and Childhood Sexual Abuse.* Minneapolis, Minnesota: Omni Recovery, 1990.

Retreat Centers

Jensen, John and Mary. *U.S. and Worldwide Guide to Retreat Center Guest Houses.* PO Box 8355, Newport Beach, CA 92660: CTS Publications, 1992.

Kelly, Marcia, and Jack Kelly. *Sanctuaries: The Northeast.* New York: Bell Tower/Crown Publishers, 1991.

——. *Sanctuaries: The West Coast and Southwest.* New York: Bell Tower/Crown Publishers, 1993.

Periodicals

Common Boundary. Circulation Department, PO Box 445, Mt. Morris, IL 61054.

Weavings: A Journal of the Christian Spiritual Life. The Upper Room, 1908 Grand Avenue, Nashville, TN 37202.

Parabola. 656 Broadway, New York, NY 10012.

About the Author

Peg Thompson, Ph.D., offers psychotherapy, spiritual direction, consultation, and training services through her private practice in St. Paul, Minnesota. She also teaches a course on religious and spiritual development at two Twin Cities graduate schools. When not working, she can often be found birdwatching, tending her garden, or fishing in a trout stream. She lives with her partner and their two dogs in a rural setting near the Twin Cities.

Other titles that will interest you:

Daybreak
Meditations for Women Survivors of Sexual Abuse
by Maureen Brady
Childhood sexual abuse is a haunting experience—an experience often filled with silence and secrecy. These 366 supportive meditations offer you comfort and wisdom in your courageous journey toward healing and wholeness. 400 pp.
Order No. 5053

A Life of My Own
Daily Meditations on Hope and Acceptance
by the author of Each Day a New Beginning
Direct and affirming, these 366 meditations gently guide you to a better understanding of yourself and your relationships with chemically dependent family members, co-Otehr.workers, and friends. Messages focus on Twelve Step principles such as living in the present, detaching with love, and asking for help. 400 pp.
Order No. 1070

For price and order information, or a free catalog, please call our
Telephone Representatives

HAZELDEN

1-800-328-0098   1-651-213-4000   1-651-257-1331
(24-hours Toll-Free. U.S.,   *(outside the U.S*   *(24 Hours Fax)*
Canada & the Virgin Islands)   *& Canada)*

Pleasent Valley Road • P. O. Box 176 • Center City, MN 55012-0176

http://www.hazelden.org